Yes, Boys Can!

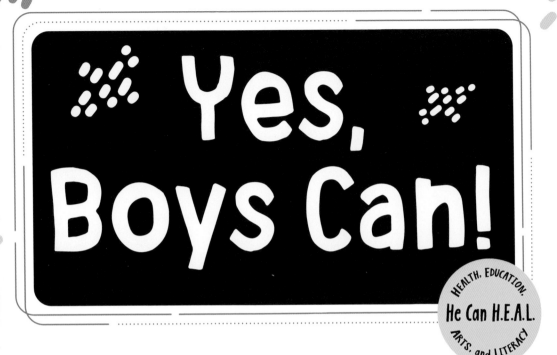

Yes, Boys Can!

HEALTH, EDUCATION, He Can H.E.A.L. ARTS, and LITERACY

Inspiring Stories of Men Who Changed the World

JONATHAN JURAVICH

2023 National Elementary Art Teacher of the Year

RICHARD V. REEVES

Founder of the American Institute for Boys and Men

ILLUSTRATIONS BY CHRIS KING

QUARRY

Quarto.com

© 2024 Quarto Publishing Group USA Inc.
Text © 2024 Jonathan Juravich and
Richard V. Reeves

First Published in 2024 by Quarry Books,
an imprint of The Quarto Group,
100 Cummings Center, Suite 265-D,
Beverly, MA 01915, USA.
T (978) 282-9590 F (978) 283-2742

Quarry Books titles are also available at discount
for retail, wholesale, promotional, and bulk
purchase. For details, contact the Special Sales
Manager by email at specialsales@quarto.com or
by mail at The Quarto Group, Attn: Special Sales
Manager, 100 Cummings Center, Suite 265-D,
Beverly, MA 01915, USA.

10 9 8 7 6 5 4 3 2 1

ISBN: 978-07603-9195-2

Digital edition published in 2024
eISBN: 978-07603-9196-9

Library of Congress Cataloging-in-Publication
Data is available.

Design and Page Layout: Megan Jones Design
Illustration: Chris King

Printed in Malaysia

For Ari and Josie, who remind me to seek joy in life's small moments.
—JJ

For Bryce, an inspiring educator and cherished son.
— RR

Contents

60
YU "PHILLIP" XU
Nurse

63
MO WILLEMS
Author
Illustrator

64
KWAME ALEXANDER
Poet and Author

67
DEAN VENDRAMIN
Teacher

68
KURT RUSSELL
Teacher

71
DANIEL VIJAYARAJ
Nurse

72
CARLOS ACOSTA
Dancer

75
STEPHEN WILTSHIRE
Visual Artist

76
MIGUEL CARDONA
Teacher

79
COREY BULMAN
Teacher

80
BABAK
MASHHADI EBRAHIM
Teacher

83
PETER TABICHI
Teacher

84
LUKE HAYNES
Quilter

87
CANDIDO CRESPO
Teacher
Visual Artist

88
JERMAR ROUNTREE
Teacher

91
EDDIE WOO
Teacher

92
WILL POOLEY
Nurse

95
RANJITSINH DISALE
Teacher

96
CURTIS OLAND
Fashion Designer

99
HENRY LIANG
Flutist

100
RUFAI ZAKARI
Visual Artist

103
TAKERU "TK"
NAGAYOSHI
Teacher

104
TOM DALEY
Knitter

107
KEVIN ASPAAS
Weaver

108
ADRIAN BERMUDEZ
Nurse

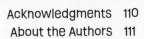

Health   Education   Arts   Literacy

Introduction

My youngest son, Cameron, was about six. I was driving him home after seeing the doctor. We were quiet for a time. Then he said, "Dad, I didn't know men could be doctors."

The doctor we had just seen was a man. But I realized that until that day, every doctor he had ever seen had been a woman. So it was not silly for him to think that being a doctor was something only women did.

But stop to consider this for a moment. That's amazing progress. Women were not even allowed to be doctors for most of human history! For women to be the only doctors in Cameron's world shows how relatively quickly and overwhelmingly stereotypes can be overcome.

I told Cameron then, and I am telling you now, yes, men can be doctors! But just as important, men can be *nurses*, too. Maybe that one sounds strange to you because most nurses are still women. But there are thousands of amazing nurses who are men. It is a great job for a man, and do not let anybody tell you otherwise! There are no rules about what jobs men can do.

This book is about the sorts of jobs that are sometimes wrongly seen as jobs for women but are just as much for men.

Men like Joe Hogan, who wanted to be a nurse but was told he was not allowed to be. That was because the nearby college teaching nursing only admitted women! In 1982 the Supreme Court said the school had to open its doors to men, and Joe got his wish.

Men like Will Pooley, who was working in Africa to save people's lives from the Ebola virus when he got sick with the disease himself. Once he had recovered, what did Will do? He went back to Africa to carry on his work.

Men like Hector Hugo Gonzalez, who served in the Vietnam War and ended up as president of the National Association of Hispanic Nurses in 1982.

Back during that car ride with Cameron, we talked about teachers. There were no men teaching at his elementary school, so he was not sure men could do that job either. In most countries, fewer men are teaching today than they used to. In the United States, only 23 percent of teachers are men now, compared with 33 percent in 1980.

But men can be teachers! In fact, I think we need men teaching and coaching in our schools more than ever.

Maybe you are more interested in STEM jobs, in which case, great! But maybe not. Maybe you are more interested in working with people, which is great, too. These are what I call "HEAL" subjects and jobs: in health, education, arts, and literacy. Nurses, teachers, childcare workers, therapists, social workers, assistants, psychologists: These are all HEAL jobs.

In recent years, girls have been encouraged to believe that they can be anything they want. That includes jobs that people once thought were "men's jobs." Now there are almost as many women as men working as doctors, lawyers, and scientists. Women fly fighter planes, fight fires, and pass laws. Maybe you even know some of them. This is amazing and wonderful.

But adults have not done as well yet showing that men can also do the things that are still thought of as "women's jobs," mostly in those HEAL professions. Just like girls used to be told that math or science was not right for girls, today boys too often get the message that nursing or social work or teaching are not "manly," or something equally stupid.

So, I am going to be honest with you. Right now it takes some courage to say you are thinking about one of these jobs, say, as a teacher or nurse. One of my other sons, Bryce, is a teacher, working with younger students. As a man, sometimes he has had to work extra hard to pursue this dream. He has not always been encouraged by others. But he is not going to let other people's views stop him. Nor will you, I hope.

Men can be nurses. Men can be teachers. Jermar Rountree from Washington, D.C., was a finalist for National Teacher of the Year and loves his job. He says, "I love what I do, and that will not change. I am dedicated to my kids, families, and colleagues. I want to be that trusted person, that father figure, that coach that my students can rely on no matter what."

Did you know that John Adams, the second president of the United States, was a classroom teacher? So was Archbishop Desmond Tutu, a hero to the people of South Africa for his fight for justice.

These are men who matter, whom you can count on. They offer a helping hand, not a clenched fist. They are brave men doing hard work to make life better for all of us. They are providers of care, love, practical assistance, safety, and learning.

Men can be psychologists or counselors, helping people who are sad or lonely. Men can be social workers, helping families and people who are in trouble. These are men like Warren McAdams, who went from being a volunteer firefighter to making it a career, often helping families with sick children, and men like Josh Bower, a police officer in the K9 unit working with dogs who became a counselor so that he could help people before they got into trouble, rather than afterward.

Lots of the men who choose these jobs, which some people insultingly think are "women's jobs," are proud of their work. Nurse Ben Medina says, "Nursing as a career has been such a blessing. It is a fantastic, amazing profession. Every day I'm excited to go to work."

Teachers, counselors, nurses. These men are heroes, I think, in a different but equal way to firefighters and pilots and soldiers. They know they are making a difference in other people's lives. They are pillars of strength in the lives of people who need them most. Maybe you could be one, too. Why not?

—Richard V. Reeves

Laurent Clerc

Education: Teacher

An education is based on communication. But what if there was no standardized approach to teaching, communicating, or respecting you where you lived? And what if where you lived was the United States? Enter Laurent Clerc, the first deaf teacher of the deaf in the United States.

Trauma

Laurent was born on December 26, 1785, in a small village in France. When he was one year old, he fell into a fire. The trauma resulted in a large scar on the right side of his face and a loss of both his hearing and sense of smell. Laurent had no formal schooling until he was twelve, when he enrolled in a school for deaf students in Paris. He excelled and was asked to stay with the school as an assistant teacher, and then he took on some of the most challenging courses.

The Voyage

A young man named Thomas Gallaudet traveled to Europe to learn about deaf education and bring back teaching methods to the United States. He was frustrated by his experience until he met Laurent. Thomas studied with Laurent, learning about sign language and how the Parisian school for deaf students operated. Thomas and Laurent worked well together and became friends. When it was time for Thomas to take his learning back to the United States, Laurent was persuaded to come along. During the long voyage, Thomas learned sign language from Laurent, and Laurent learned English from Thomas.

Sign Language

The two men created their own school for the deaf in Hartford, Connecticut. Thomas was the school's principal. Laurent was busy at the school. He taught Thomas, the students, and hearing men who wanted to study deaf education. In the United States at the time, there was no standard sign language used by the deaf community. Students came to the school with signs they developed at home or within their local community. So, when Laurent taught his students, he used what he knew best: French Sign Language. His students would take this learning and blend it with their own signs. Laurent's influence was so significant that these signs became popular and ultimately became American Sign Language (ASL). Today, about two-thirds of ASL signs are linked to French Sign Language and Laurent.

Many Firsts

In 1818, when it was time to seek more funding for deaf education and their school, Laurent went to Washington, D.C., becoming the first deaf person to stand in front of Congress. The next day, he became the first deaf person to meet the president of the United States at the White House. His visits persuaded Congress to eventually pass a bill that would offer financial stability to the school. When Laurent first left France to follow Thomas, he said he would come, but only briefly. But during his time in the United States, he helped form a revolutionary school, inspired ASL, started a family, and changed how the United States viewed deaf education. Laurent passed away on July 18, 1869.

Go Give It a Try!

Have you ever tried to learn ASL? There are books, virtual resources, and probably even local classes you can attend to learn this language that is distinctly its own. ASL is not a signed representation of English; it has its own sentence structure that does not follow the rules of the spoken English language.

Walt Whitman

Health: Nurse
Literacy: Poet

Sometimes, when someone is recognized for one aspect of their life, this one role overshadows their other important accomplishments. For example, Walt Whitman, one of the most important American poets of all time, was also a nurse. His experiences with patients influenced his poetry.

Unhappy Childhood

Walt was born on May 31, 1819, on Long Island, New York. He once remarked that he didn't have a happy childhood, with a family often stressed about how they would survive financially. To help with the family's income, he left school to find work at the age of eleven. Walt had several jobs, including as a teacher and a journalist.

Poetry for Everyone

In 1855 he published his first book of poems and started to become well-known for his poetry. He wrote poems about nature, friendship, and love. His goal was to write poetry for everyday Americans. Walt's book of poetry was revised, edited, and released several times during his lifetime.

The Civil War

When the Civil War broke out, Walt's brother George joined the Union army. One day, Walt was reading a newspaper when he saw his brother's name on a list of wounded servicemen. He immediately went to find him. When Walt found his brother—who had only minor wounds to his face—he saw so many other sick and wounded men. He decided that he had to be a part of helping these men at their lowest moments.

Volunteer Nurse

During the Civil War, Walt got a full-time job in Washington, D.C., but spent all his spare time as a volunteer nurse in army hospitals. At the beginning of Walt's time as a volunteer nurse, he brought candy and fruit to the injured soldiers and sat with them to hear their stories. He wrote letters for the soldiers to their families. He eventually cared for their battle wounds. After hearing their stories, Walt wrote poetry about his patients and sometimes mentioned the care he provided. Walt, a fan of President Lincoln, also wrote some of his most famous poems reflecting on the president's death.

Popularity

Though his poetry grew in popularity during his lifetime, it wasn't until his death that Walt's works were recognized more broadly. Walt passed away on March 26, 1892. Today, he is considered one of the greatest American poets of all time.

Go Give It a Try!

Our life experiences can inspire the creation of poetry. Consider an event from your life that was joyful, or a difficult and challenging experience, and write a poem that focuses on the five senses. What did you see, smell, touch, hear, and taste during this moment? Remember, the poem doesn't need to rhyme but should be an expression of one of your experiences.

Joseph Lee
Arts: Culinary Arts/Baker

Bread is not something we spend a lot of time thinking about, as it is ever present in packed lunches, alongside meals, or on its own slathered with butter. We have one baker, Joseph Lee, to thank for our ability to have delicious, cost-effective bread.

Born Enslaved
Joseph was born in 1948 in Charleston, South Carolina. His parents were both enslaved, and so was Joseph. He grew up in South Carolina, learning to bake as a child while working at a bakery. Joseph didn't ever have a formal education, but he did go to some underground schools whenever he was able to. During the Civil War, he became a blacksmith, using heat to form metal. Then, Joseph became a cook on a ship, making his way north while improving his cooking and baking skills.

Baking as a Career
In Massachusetts, Joseph took a job in a bakery while selling food out of the boardinghouse where he lived. His breads and the other foods he created were delicious, and people took notice. Joseph opened his own restaurant while he was still in his twenties and began developing the Woodland Park Hotel in Newton, Massachusetts. The hotel was a resort getaway that grew in popularity and brought in wealthy and famous visitors, including three presidents.

Better, Quicker Bread
A skilled baker, Joseph wanted to create better, more delicious, and more efficient bread for his hotel. He set to work, dreaming up an invention that would take the strain and pain off the bakers he was working with and still produce a great product. Joseph developed an automated bread-kneading machine that saved time and resulted in better-quality bread.

Too Much Bread
Then the unthinkable happened: There was too much bread! With the help of Joseph's new invention, there was more bread than the staff could serve and his guests could eat. Joseph got to work again, inventing the automatic bread-crumbing machine. The day-old bread that would have been wasted was instead crumbled up to be reused in new ways. Modern-day breadcrumbs are used for frying fish, stuffing turkeys, or topping salads as croutons.

Long Overdue
Joseph sold his inventions to other companies, which made the baking industry even more efficient and cost-effective while limiting human failures often associated with baking bread. But his impact on the world was largely forgotten after his death in 1908. Then, in 2019 Joseph was inducted into the National Inventors Hall of Fame, noting his role in the great legacy of baking.

Go Give It a Try!
Research how to make a loaf of bread. With the help of an adult, gather the ingredients and tools and try creating the bread by hand. As you do, pay attention to the muscles you use to create one loaf.

Booker T. Washington
Education: Teacher

Sometimes, our actions and choices can lead to greatness and growth for others. And yet, at other times, our words and decisions can be revisited with a new lens that results in controversy. That is the story of Booker T. Washington, the son of an enslaved woman, who became a teacher and a champion for industrial education.

Emancipation

Booker was born on April 5, 1856, in Hale's Ford, Virginia, to an enslaved woman who worked as a cook for a plantation owner. After emancipation (when enslaved people in the United States were given their freedom), Booker's mother moved her family to West Virginia.

Hard Work

At the age of nine, Booker worked packing salt and then in a coal mine. He could go to school, but only after his work laboring with salt or coal was complete. But Booker desired even more education. When he was older, he walked five hundred miles (805 km) from his home to what is now known as Hampton University. He made the journey almost all by foot and with no money. Booker got a job as a janitor to pay for his education at the university.

A Foundation for Tuskegee

After graduation, Booker taught kids at a school during the day and adults at night. When he was twenty-five years old, he was selected to lead a new school for other African Americans. The school is now internationally known as Tuskegee University. Booker's new school, where he led and taught, had two small buildings, no equipment, and very little money. When he passed away thirty-four years later, there were one hundred well-equipped buildings, a thousand-plus students, a large faculty, and the funds to continue the work he had begun.

Communication and Controversy

Booker took pride in his ability to debate and communicate his opinions. However, his views on desegregation (the ending of laws that separated Black and white people) were controversial. While other leaders in the Black community were speaking out against segregation and focusing on the beginnings of the civil rights movement, Booker wanted African Americans to focus more on their economic advancement, which angered other Black leaders. He wanted his fellow African Americans to work toward financial security by pursuing an education that developed their industrial and farming skills instead of focusing on their rights as citizens.

Recognition and Legacy

During his lifetime, Booker wrote a dozen books. In 1901 he was the first African American to be invited to dinner at the White House by President Theodore Roosevelt. Booker died on November 14, 1915. Today, his school, Tuskegee University, continues a legacy of success. The university is now the nation's number one educator of African American aerospace engineers. Booker's legacy has been controversial. His focus on education was admirable, though others have challenged his views as offsetting the civil rights movement and limiting the advancement of Black individuals in the United States.

Go Give It a Try!

To fully understand how far Booker T. Washington walked to get an education, use digital resources to search what is located five hundred miles (805 km) from your home. What cities, sites, and possibilities are that far from you? Have you ever been to any of these locations? And now imagine walking that distance.

John Dewey
Education: Teacher

Could doing chores actually be a learning experience? That is what educational philosopher John Dewey believed. He even designed a whole school around the idea that when we complete chores, we learn new skills, including how to be a member of a community.

Early Life
John was born on October 20, 1859, in Burlington, Vermont. He attended the public schools in Burlington, where he excelled. At the young age of fifteen, John became a student at the University of Vermont. His favorite topic to study was philosophy, which is studying knowledge itself: how humans think and how things work. When John graduated four years later, he was second in his class.

Research and Teaching
John taught in Pennsylvania and then in his home state of Vermont. While teaching, he continued to study philosophy, having in-depth conversations with his former teacher. He decided to continue his education and further study philosophy at universities, later taking on the role of teacher in the philosophy department at several universities.

Think Creatively
Based on his studies, John believed that humans rely on their habits in their day-to-day lives, but when changes occur, they are forced to think creatively to regain control. He insisted that education had to change and be available to everyone. John thought that students at a young age needed to learn to break free of their normal habits and think creatively for themselves.

An Experimental School
In 1894 John and his wife Harriet started an experimental primary school in Chicago where John could test out his educational ideas. His own children attended the school. John believed that kids learned best by doing. He criticized schools for focusing too much on preparing kids for later life when they should be learning for their lives now. John understood that for real learning to occur, students had to feel involved and see how their learning was relevant to their lives.

Community
Through his work at the primary school, John believed that classrooms should be communities where students work together and help one another. He strongly encouraged students to take on chores at school, which helped them understand their ability to contribute to the greater society. Specifically, John believed that chores should not be assigned by gender—all students should learn to sew and cook, not just girls.

Legacy
John died on June 1, 1952, and left a rich legacy of educational thinking. Though John's ideas have also been misunderstood, misapplied, or completely dismissed by others as too wild and not centered on academic success, his research changed education, with his ideas adopted in countless classrooms around the globe.

Go Give It a Try!
The next time you are asked to help with chores at school or home, take a minute to think about how you are contributing to the classroom or your family. What is now possible for everyone because of your work? And what did you learn by completing your chores? Why not offer to take care of a chore before you are asked?

Forrest Spaulding
Literacy: Librarian

Walking into a library is magical—shelves and shelves of books of limitless topics and genres. There are books for almost every age and every interest. But what if that wasn't true? In the 1930s librarian Forrest Spaulding experienced the beginnings of censorship (when words or ideas are kept from others) and wanted to ensure that everyone had access to literature. His Library Bill of Rights proclaimed that everyone should have access to books.

Library School

Forrest was born on May 4, 1892, in Nashua, New Hampshire. As a young man, he moved to New York City and worked as a newspaper reporter. He then attended the New York Public Library's library school in 1913. Forrest began working in libraries in New York and New Jersey until moving to Des Moines, Iowa, becoming the city's librarian.

First Time in Iowa

While serving as the city's librarian, Forrest saw the importance of getting books into the hands of those with limited access, including men in the military. He organized a library at Camp Dodge in Iowa for World War I recruits. He then set up military camp libraries in other states. Forrest provided the soldiers with books on a wide range of topics and wanted all the books to be returned well used. In 1920 Forrest moved to the country of Peru. He oversaw the country's libraries and museums while working as a reporter for the Associated Press.

Back to Iowa

While in Peru, Forrest worked to provide news from the country but was often met with censorship. In 1927 he returned to his role as the Des Moines Public Library director and brought with him new and creative ideas, such as recording library programs for the radio airwaves. As the Great Depression hit the country, Forrest did his best to make books available to everyone and established the "Waterfront University" in the library's basement. This wasn't a real university but a place where men without work could find resources to further their technical and job-related learning.

The Library Bill of Rights

Forrest became angered by the United States's first censorship of library books. Elsewhere in the world, books were being banned and burned in great numbers because of their content. In 1938 Forrest drafted the Library Bill of Rights, which focused on an unbiased (without opinion) book selection, a balanced collection, and open meeting rooms. The library board accepted Forrest's statements and proclaimed they would not be bullied into censorship. Soon after, the American Library Association adopted the Library Bill of Rights for the nation. Though the document has been edited and updated based on current advances, the basic principles continue to this day. Forrest died on December 9, 1965, living a life dedicated to books and the freedom of expression and learning.

Go Give It a Try!

Do you have a library card for your local library? Start by getting one; it is free and easy. Learn about all the benefits of your card beyond checking out physical books. Many libraries have events, guest speakers, technology and equipment rentals, study spaces, tutoring, and digital downloads of audiobooks—and yes, books, access to a world of books. Visit your local library today.

Dr. Alfred Mayer Neumann

Health: Social Worker

If you are narrowly escaping death because of who you are, you would probably be thinking about survival, making it through the next few days. Or would you begin to think about how you had been given a new opportunity to support so many others? This is how Dr. Alfred Mayer Neumann viewed his life after escaping the unthinkable. He had a new chance to positively impact the lives of others.

Supporting the Community

Alfred was born in 1910 in Vienna, Austria. He earned a law degree from the University of Vienna. When Hitler and the Nazis began their occupation (takeover) of Austria, Alfred worked as a counselor and organized resources for Jewish families in need. He helped get them emergency housing, set up programs for learning new trades for work, and dealt with immigration problems. He became a critical part of the Jewish community's survival.

Escape from Austria

In 1938 Alfred was scheduled to be sent to Dachau, a Nazi death camp. His mother pleaded with and ultimately bribed the officials, who gave Alfred seventy-two hours to leave the country. And like that, Alfred was running for his life, ultimately making it to the United States. In New York City, he attended school for social work. He had already been doing this work in Austria, but now he was receiving formal education on the topic.

Supporting the Displaced

As a social worker, Alfred worked in several states supporting vulnerable communities, especially those taken from their homes, an experience he knew all too well. Eventually, Alfred made it to Denver, where he served as the executive director and vice president of the Jewish Family and Children's Service of Colorado. He completely re-envisioned the family counseling program and developed new initiatives focused on adoptions and immigration services.

SHALOM

Used as a greeting, the word *shalom* means "peace." Beginning in 1954, Alfred worked with several others to create a program called SHALOM Denver that supported Holocaust survivors and later included refugees of other conflicts around the world. Reimagining his work in Vienna, Alfred's team provided housing, employment, job training, and the necessary social and emotional support their clients desperately needed.

Celebrate

On June 30, 1982, the Colorado governor proclaimed that it was Dr. Alfred M. Neumann Day. Later, Alfred was named a Social Work Pioneer by the National Association of Social Workers. Alfred passed away on March 3, 2002. This pioneer and advocate for displaced people wanted nothing more than to live a life that improved human existence, and he had done just that and more.

Go Give It a Try!

June 30, 1982, was Dr. Alfred M. Neumann Day. Honor someone incredible in your life with a day just for them, and no, not their birthday. Create a certificate for them, offer a special meal, and possibly even put up decorations. Celebrate all that they do for you and others. Not only will they be overwhelmed with joy but you will be, too.

John Myron Rockmore
Health: Social Worker

A pioneer is someone who has original ideas and helps open new possibilities for others. They are often leaders who inspire others to join their cause or champion their ideas. John Myron Rockmore was a pioneer in the field of social work. He envisioned and advocated (fought) for the importance of social workers in supporting those with mental illness, especially those in the military.

Diplomas and Degrees

John was born in 1913 in Brooklyn, New York. He attended college and graduated with an education degree. In 1939 John received a diploma from the New York School of Social Work, today known as the Columbia University School of Social Work. He worked for the New York Department of Social Services and the Education Bureau until World War II broke out.

Military Service

During the war, John became the chief of military psychiatric social work in the army's first-ever "mental hygiene unit." He worked as a psychiatric social worker, a special kind of social worker who supports people who have intense mental health needs. This may mean coordinating their care, providing therapy, or making sure they are hospitalized. Those serving in the military had mental health needs just like other people but had the additional impacts of the war bearing down on them.

Consulting

When World War II ended, John became a consultant to the Surgeon General of the U.S. Army. His advice became essential in expanding access to social work programs within the military and establishing policies in the new world of mental health support. John was very proud of his time in the army and was awarded a medal and Citation for Legion of Merit for his work to support mental health programs for military members. The Legion of Merit is an award in the U.S. military given to individuals for exceptional service and achievements.

Necessary Treatment

John worked as the director of social services at a treatment center in New York, taught at Columbia University, and later became the first director of social services for the Connecticut Department of Mental Health. He continued at the Department of Mental Health for twenty-three years. Over time, John helped to make social work be seen as a necessary part of mental health treatment alongside nursing and psychiatry. He advocated that social workers who focused on mental health care would also need to provide counseling and resources to family members of those being treated for mental illness, as well as the importance of aftercare. He wrote more than eighty articles on social work and mental health. John died on October 12, 2002, leaving behind a legacy of care and support for those struggling with mental health in and out of the military.

Go Give It a Try!

The U.S. Department of Veterans Affairs (VA) has hospitals around the nation supporting the physical and mental health of military veterans. Locate which VA hospital is closest to you and create a gratitude poster for the patients, complete with an image and inspirational words. Deliver the poster to the hospital for the staff to display for the patients.

Luther Christman

Health: Nurse

Leader. Trailblazer. Legend. Icon. These words were used to describe Luther Christman later in his life. But this isn't how his story began. His story, a lesson in overcoming challenges, reminds us not to give up. Sometimes you just need to change your approach.

Denied Access

Luther, the son of a coal miner, was born on February 26, 1915, in Summit Hill, Pennsylvania. He was interested in a future as a nurse. And it didn't take long for him to face resistance. He was a man trying to join a field comprised of mostly women. When World War II broke out, Luther wanted to serve his country and tried to join the Army Nurse Corps. The Corps did not allow him to join because he was a man. He later applied to two different university programs and was refused admission for the same reason. Luther was called names because of his desire to be a nurse.

A New Tactic

Though some of the challenges that Luther faced would make many people give up on their goals, it made him only more determined to be a part of a field he believed in. Instead, he tried a new strategy and worked and did research in psychology. That led to leadership roles at several university nursing programs. His desire to join nursing led him to become a leader who would change the field from the inside.

Advocacy and Inclusivity

Throughout his leadership in university settings, Luther advocated (fought) for men to be included into the nursing profession. He also believed that the field should include everyone who wanted to serve those who were most vulnerable and in need of health care. As the first male dean of the School of Nursing at Vanderbilt University, he became the first dean to hire African American women as faculty members.

Elevating the Profession

As a leader, Luther sought to elevate the profession with strong standards of excellence for all nurses. His belief was that nurses could give the best care to their patients with access to continual education and learning from practicing nurses at the university level. He wanted to provide nurses more time with their patients. His idea was to give administrative assistants the non-nursing tasks that nurses may have traditionally taken care of.

Recognition

In 1974 Luther helped institute the National Male Nurse Association, which later became the American Assembly for Men in Nursing. In 2004 he was the first man admitted into the American Nursing Association's Hall of Fame. Then, in 2007, the association established the Luther Christman Award to recognize men who significantly contributed to the nursing profession. Luther died on June 7, 2011. From his complicated beginnings trying to join nursing, Luther went on to positively influence and uplift the profession for nurses everywhere.

Go Give It a Try!

Not every nurse in your life will be named to the Nursing Hall of Fame. Take time to recognize someone you know in the nursing community for their efforts. Create a video, make a social media post, or send a message to show your appreciation for their inspiring work.

Arthur George Smith

Arts: Jewelry Artist

Where do artists find their inspiration for their masterful works of art? Inspiration can come from anywhere: nature, our experiences, the people in our lives, and the world around us. Artist Arthur George Smith's jewelry designs found their beginnings in sculpture and dance.

Early Recognition

Arthur, known as Art, was born in 1917 in Cuba to parents who had emigrated from Jamaica. At the age of three, the family moved to New York City. At a young age, he showed artistic talent. In the eighth grade, Art won an honorable mention in a poster contest sponsored by the American Society for the Prevention of Cruelty to Animals. He was encouraged to attend art school, and he did, receiving a scholarship.

Inspired

In art school, Art was one of a small number of Black students. His advisers tried to push him to pursue architecture, suggesting he could get a job more easily in that profession. However, the mathematical precision of this field wasn't interesting to Art. He instead focused on sculpture. Upon graduating from art school, Art began taking night classes in jewelry making. Art became friends with another Black jewelry designer, Winifred Mason, who became his mentor and hired Art as a full-time assistant. Now, Art could learn alongside someone successful in this field who even owned their own studio and store. Art was inspired.

On His Own

In 1946 Art decided to make his move and opened his own jewelry studio and shop on a street with primarily Italian neighbors. He suffered racial violence from his neighbors, who threatened him, made him feel unwanted, and smashed his store windows. Art moved his shop to a new, more inclusive neighborhood, and his business thrived. Not only was he selling his work in his store, but his artistic jewelry was sold in craft stores in multiple cities. In the 1950s major retailers such as Bloomingdale's made his work available to a broader public.

Dance

The jewelry that Art designed was big and sculptural. The world of dance and music inspired him. He was hired to design jewelry pieces for innovative Black dance companies. His work got even bigger and more theatrical, featuring silver hand hammered into creative forms. The dancers' bodies made his designs come to life. Significant fashion magazines, including *Vogue*, featured Art's designs. Art even had the remarkable opportunity to design a brooch for First Lady Eleanor Roosevelt and cuff links for the musician Duke Ellington.

Legacy

Art's health declined in the late 1970s, which brought on the closing of his shop in 1979. In 1982 he passed away. His legacy continues as his oversize sculptural jewelry pieces are a part of museum and gallery collections.

Go Give It a Try!

Gather scissors, glue or tape, string, cardboard, and items destined for the recycling bin. Consider how you will use these found materials to make large jewelry pieces like necklaces or bracelets. Who will wear these pieces: you or someone else? Get cutting, gluing, and attaching to create your own theatrical jewelry items.

Whitney Young Jr.
Health: Social Worker

One role of a social worker is to help identify supports for people who face challenges in their lives. Whitney Young Jr. didn't just work as a social worker; he lived as an advocate for those who continually battle for access to their civil rights.

Tensions and Common Ground

Whitney was born on July 31, 1921, in Lincoln Ridge, Kentucky. Whitney always dreamed of becoming a medical doctor. But from 1942 to 1944, he served in the U.S. Army, and things went in a different direction. While in the army, Whitney was part of a construction crew of Black soldiers supervised by white officers. Tensions between the two groups of men were high. Whitney worked with the two groups to come to common ground. This interaction prompted Whitney to rethink his future goals, and after the war, he set his sights on a career in social work.

The Urban League

Whitney worked with the Urban League in several states and ultimately became the executive director of the National Urban League for ten years. The Urban League is an organization that supports African Americans and other underserved urban residents. When Whitney stepped into his role, the association was centered more on providing services and addressing middle-class issues. Whitney realized that his desire was for the organization to get involved with direct action and focus on the needs of poor people in the city. Under his leadership, the organization became a leader in the civil rights movement.

Collaboration and Action

The Urban League's active role in the American civil rights movement, under the leadership of Whitney, led to the organization's involvement in planning the March on Washington for Jobs and Freedom, where Martin Luther King Jr. delivered the now famous "I Have a Dream" speech. Whitney spoke that day, pleading with attendees to not just show up to march but to take action for their civil rights. Whitney and Martin were friends and collaborators, meeting with government leaders. Whitney himself advised and worked with several U.S. presidents on the topics of race, urban communities, and war.

Architecture

Whitney advocated for more people of color to join the architecture profession so that they could respond to their communities' needs. He spoke at national meetings of architects and challenged the inequality in housing available to people living in the city. Whitney called for architects to be more involved in social issues and use their work to respond to what communities of color required.

The Medal of Freedom

In 1969 Whitney was awarded the Medal of Freedom, the highest civilian award the United States has to offer. President Lyndon B. Johnson awarded him this honor based on his remarkable accomplishments focused on civil rights. Whitney passed away unexpectedly on March 11, 1971. This loss was felt throughout the country, and President Nixon spoke at his funeral. After his death, awards were created in his honor, his portrait was included on a postage stamp, and the university where he received his education in social work renamed the school in his name.

Go Give It a Try!

Architects are a significant part of our lives. They design houses, offices, schools, restaurants—any building you see. Use blocks, plastic bricks, or common household objects to create a city. Consider the purpose of each building and its location based on the other buildings.

Edward F. Krise

Health: Social Worker

Can you really make progress as a team if you are not open to understanding and empathizing with your teammates? This was the question at the center of Edward F. Krise's work as a social worker in the military and within the broader community.

Military Enlistment

Edward was born on June 28, 1924, in Detroit. He grew up in Washington, D.C. Edward later enrolled as a university student in Rhode Island, where he attended a single semester until he joined the U.S. Army. He served in World War II as a tank driver in North Africa, then went on to fight in Italy. During the Battle of Anzio, an attack by the Allies in Italy, Edward was taken prisoner. He spent fourteen months in a prison in Germany until he escaped.

Back to School

After World War II, Edward returned to university life and graduated with a degree in sociology. He then went on to study at the University of Chicago. While in Chicago, Edward lived at the Hull House, a settlement house that supported the local community in need and whose staff received international recognition for their work. While there, Edward participated in many community activities, learning firsthand the importance of social workers connecting with those in need, helping in crises, and building community.

Then, Back into the Military

To kick off his career in social work, Edward became the executive secretary of the North Dakota Youth Council, that is, until the Korean War broke out, calling Edward back into active duty. In 1951 he became an officer with the Army Medical Services Corps. He was one of the first social work officers in a newly established military-based social work program.

Battling Racism

As a social worker, Edward was responsible for crisis intervention and the role of relationships in supporting military effectiveness. It is with this lens that he became the first leader of the Department of Defense Race Relations Institute. Beginning in 1970, he worked to dismantle racism from within the military through education, relationships, and awareness of the history of racism in the United States. He believed that for a functioning team to be successful in military combat, service members had to be able to trust and value one another. His work included partnering Black and white soldiers throughout their time in the Institute and having teams complete community service activities together.

Recognition

Edward received significant recognition throughout his military service, including a Bronze Star, a Purple Heart, and a Silver Star for "Gallantry in Action." He was twice awarded the Legion of Merit for his work on race relations. The National Association of Social Workers presented him with the Social Work Pioneers Award for his creative work within the profession he cared so deeply about. Edward passed away on December 4, 2003.

Go Give It a Try!

Conflicts happen; they are a part of relationships. The next time you face a conflict, before reacting, start by calming your mind and body with breathing exercises, such as "elevator breathing." Breathe in, imagining you are going up the floors of a tall building. Then take another breath and slowly release it at each "floor." When you reach the "top," take one last big breath and slowly exhale, imagining you are taking the elevator back down to the lobby, feeling your whole body relax.

Jaime Escalante

Education: Teacher

What is possible when you believe in others and their potential, and they believe it, too? And what about when everyone else sees them as unmotivated and without a promising future? You come alongside them and make them believe they can achieve whatever they set their sights on.

In Their Footsteps

Jaime Escalante was born on December 31, 1930, in La Paz, Bolivia, to two parents who were teachers. He followed in their footsteps, teaching math and physics in Bolivia for twelve years before deciding to move to the United States. He came to the United States with only three thousand dollars and the English words "yes" and "no" in his vocabulary. But what Jaime had was perseverance.

Perseverance

Though Jaime was a teacher in Bolivia, he couldn't get a job in the United States as a teacher without getting different degrees and learning English. To put himself through school, he mopped floors in a coffee shop and then was promoted to cook. Later he was a technician for an electrical company. All the while, Jaime was learning English and taking classes in math and physics. When he was forty-three, he took a pay cut to begin his first teaching job in the United States at Garfield High School in Los Angeles.

High Standards

Jaime had high standards for himself, as he had clearly shown his whole life, but he also had high standards for his students and those around him. But at Garfield, he was given the lowest-level math classes where it was clear no one had any hopes for his students to succeed, including the students themselves. Though Jaime felt like giving up, his new mission was to motivate those who were seen as lacking ambition. He became the ultimate performer in class, telling jokes and using props to help his students understand challenging math concepts. He even required students to answer a homework question before entering the classroom, ensuring they had done their work at home to be ready to learn together.

Advanced Placement Success

But Jaime envisioned more for his students; he designed an AP (Advanced Placement) calculus course, starting with only a handful of students each year. In 1982 eighteen of his students passed the difficult AP calculus exam, resulting in a major celebration. However, the students' scores were challenged, and Jaime and his students were accused of cheating. He again saw this as the broader community not believing in the power of his students, but he believed in them. The students retook the test, with most of the students passing the challenging test yet again.

Recognition

Educators from around the country came to his school to watch the engaging way that Jaime made math come alive for his students. He received several national awards. An award-winning movie was even produced about his efforts in the classroom. Jaime died on March 30, 2010, due to cancer. After his death, the United States Postal Service released a stamp in his honor.

Go Give It a Try!

The Postal Service often recognizes individuals for their work with a stamp designed in their honor. Who in your life would you design a stamp for? Review recent stamp designs online and create a stamp recognizing this everyday hero in your life, using paper and drawing materials or digital resources. Though you won't be able to use the stamp to send the letter, be sure to present them with their honor.

Hector Hugo Gonzalez
Health: Nurse

Sometimes, barriers prevent us from reaching our full potential or pursuing a job that would better our whole lives. Hector Hugo Gonzalez saw the obstacles for people who wanted to help others and did something about it.

Deep Roots

Hector is proud of his family's deep roots in Mexico, which date back to Spanish settlers in the mid-1700s. He remarked on his family's legacy in Mexico, saying they were there "before Mexico was Mexico, before Texas was Texas, and before the United States was the United States!" Hector himself was born on March 9, 1937, in Roma, Texas.

Education

Hector studied nursing in San Antonio in the 1960s. Male nurses were so rare then that his nursing school didn't even have a restroom for men. He went on to earn a master's degree and then entered the Army Nurse Corps. He served for two years and obtained the rank of captain. Later, while teaching, Hector pursued a PhD In 1974 he was the first Mexican American registered nurse to earn a doctorate.

Removing Barriers

When he became the chairman of the Department of Nursing Education at San Antonio College, Hector had a new vision for educating nurses. He wanted to remove all barriers holding people back from pursuing a career as a nurse. He designed a two-year nursing program that was seen as revolutionary at the time. The program was flexible and offered courses entirely at night. This decision allowed those with children or other jobs to attend school and earn their degree. Students could attend classes full-time or take it slower and go part-time. He secured the largest amount of private money for nursing scholarships ever at the college. Today, a scholarship fund in his name continues to make nursing school a possibility for male nursing students who may need financial assistance. With Hector in this leadership position, removing barriers to education, San Antonio College had one of the highest numbers of male and minority nursing students in the country.

Celebrating Students

Not only did Hector remove barriers for students in the nursing program but he also saw value in uplifting students in all areas of education. When he devised his new plans for nursing at San Antonio College, he invited art students to design a new logo for the nursing program. The college used the winning logo, which also won several design awards.

Go Give It a Try!

Are you part of a club or group that could use a new logo? It's time you designed one! Think about what colors and images could represent the club. Look at some of your favorite logos for teams, stores, or restaurants. Use hands-on materials or a digital resource to design your logo and begin using it to gain interest in what your club has to offer.

Preston Dyer
Health: Social Worker

There are many ways to help others, and many professions provide opportunities to better the community. But our awareness of these roles is only as broad as our experience. Preston Dyer grew up wanting to help others, and against all odds and hurdles, he ended up becoming one of the most influential social workers alive.

Sermons and Church Services

Preston was born on April 28, 1938, in Atlanta. Growing up, the only person that Preston really saw helping other people was the pastor of his church. Preston loved the idea of helping others; it was what drove him. He wasn't excited about writing and preaching sermons for church services. It was helping people that inspired him. Preston applied to Baylor University in Texas to become a pastor with the support of his mom, who had been secretly saving for his college education for years.

A Change in Plans

Preston's grades weren't the best, but thanks to glowing references, he was admitted to the college on probation. This meant he didn't meet all the school's entry requirements but could be admitted and work hard to earn a permanent place there. At school, Preston met with an adviser who suggested he investigate other careers that focused on service beyond being a pastor. He landed on social work, especially supporting people with mental health needs. His parents were not happy with this decision; they had their own views of what a social worker did and what their son's life would be like. But Preston was focused on the good he could do for others, especially in mental health.

Probation

When it was time for graduate school, Preston was again admitted on probation. He worked hard and graduated with great grades and a master of social work degree. Preston spent several years working in Louisiana and Georgia until he received a call from Baylor University. Officials at the college Preston had graduated from were calling him back to develop a complete social work program.

The program was outstanding. Preston had done remarkable work, but he needed a doctorate to stay in his position. He had so much self-doubt about applying to another school, questioning if he was a good-enough student. He enrolled at Texas Woman's University, again on probation. Two years later, he graduated with top honors and a doctorate in sociology. He was the first man to receive that degree from the university.

Better Together

Preston and his wife, Genie, started marriage enrichment courses. They taught their courses around the country and to diverse audiences, including individuals without homes. Their work together prompted Genie to go back to school and earn a PhD, opening the doors for the husband-and-wife team to begin teaching a course at Baylor together. Their course focused on marriage and family sociology. It was helpful for students because they were hearing and learning from both partners in a marriage. Preston taught this course for twenty years, most of it alongside his wife. In 2014 Preston was recognized as the "most influential social worker alive" by the Social Work Degree Guide.

Go Give It a Try!

Who is an adult in your life whom you see helping other people? Interview them about what drives their mission, what types of education they received, and what goals they have for the people they work with. What does their day-to-day work look like? Use your interview to spark a conversation about this remarkable person with others.

Ronald G. Lewis
Health: Social Worker
Education: Teacher

What if your life and your interests inspired meaningful research? And what if that research went on to inform a national law that changed how generations of children were cared for and supported? Enter Ronald G. Lewis, a strong social worker, teacher, and advocate.

Unique Challenges and Joys

Ronald, a citizen of the Cherokee Nation, was born on December 3, 1941, in Muskogee, Oklahoma. As a citizen of the Cherokee Nation, Ronald grew up understanding the unique culture, challenges, and joys of being an indigenous (native) person. Striving to support people much like himself, he went to school to become a social worker. In 1974 Ronald became the first American Indian to receive a PhD in social work.

Many Firsts

Ronald was called the "Father of American Indian Social Work" and had many notable "firsts." Beyond being the first American Indian to receive a PhD in social work, he was also the first American Indian to be tenured in the University of Wisconsin system. When someone is tenured at a university, it means that they are a permanent employee and are provided certain protections. Ronald was also the first American Indian to be a full professor of social work and the first indigenous person named as a "dean" in Canada.

Teacher

Having taught at several universities, spoken around the country, and developed programs for indigenous populations, Ronald became the leading expert in American Indian social work. He researched issues that were specific to their families and communities, including the care of children and alcoholism. His research and efforts inspired many young indigenous people working at the university level.

Indian Child Welfare Act

In 1978 Ronald's research informed the creation of the Indian Child Welfare Act. This law created rules for adopting and fostering American Indian children in the United States. The law states that children born and living within an American Indian nation will continue to live within their community whenever possible. Ronald was an advocate who spoke up when he knew there was a better solution that met the needs of the American Indian people. Ronald met with members of Congress and even U.S. presidents to advocate for issues most important to him. Ronald passed away on April 14, 2019, from cancer.

Go Give It a Try!

Whose land are you on? Use an online resource to research which indigenous people originally lived where you are now living. Don't stop there: Investigate their culture further and share your learning with your family and friends.

Mikhail Baryshnikov
Arts: Dancer

It can be easy to accept that we do things as they have always been done, to stay the course and not make things too complicated. But what happens when we seek innovation (creativity) and excellence? Mikhail Baryshnikov is seen as one of the world's greatest ballet dancers, who continues to leap toward new possibilities for himself and the whole artistic community.

Early Studies

Mikhail was born on January 28, 1948, in the Soviet Union, in what is now known as the country of Latvia. His mother introduced him to the arts, including music, theater, and ballet. At the age of twelve, Mikhail began studying ballet. A few years later, he won the top prize at an international ballet competition.

Frustration and Escape

Mikhail joined the Kirov Ballet and was recognized for his incredible talent. But he was also frustrated. The ballet companies in the Soviet Union staged only performances that stuck to traditional forms of ballet and dismissed new and creative dances created by those from outside the country. Mikhail grew tired of the rules placed on him as an artist. In 1974, while touring with other dancers in Canada, Mikhail was able to escape. He declared he was never going back to the Soviet Union and was seeking asylum. Those who ask for asylum believe they are unsafe in their home country and are seeking the protection of another country. Mikhail was allowed to live in Canada and joined the ballet company there.

Dancing and Directing

Mikhail joined American ballet companies, learning from coaches and directors that only made him a stronger dancer. He had the most impressive leaping ability, allowing him to dance complicated choreography (the steps of a dance) with elegance and power. After some time, Mikhail joined the American Ballet Theatre as a dancer but also as an artistic director. An artistic director works to bring ballet performances to life, determining the vision and direction the dance company will go.

Innovation

Innovation drove Mikhail and his work. As a result, he cofounded a program called the White Oak Dance Project. This new modern dance company employed experienced dancers as part of a touring company, with Mikhail as director. Years later, Mikhail founded the Baryshnikov Arts Center in New York City. This creative space supports different types of artists to explore, create, and perform their works with artistic freedom.

Stage and Screen

Known as one of the greatest dancers of all time, Mikhail received many awards, including the National Medal of the Arts. Beyond his direction and advocacy for artistic expression, Mikhail has acted on the stage and in TV shows and movies.

Go Give It a Try!
Mikhail was an exceptional leaper. Gather friends or family for a competition to see how far you can each leap. Mark off where each person lands. Remember, the goal is to jump over a long distance and not just up.

Gregor Lersch

Arts: Floral Designer

Flowers are tied to our emotions and the big moments of our lives. The right arrangement of thoughtfully selected flowers in a particular color can bring someone to tears and remind them there is beauty in the world. Gregor Lersch knows and lives this truth. And, he is well known for being one of the greatest floral designers in the world.

Generations of Horticulturalists

Gregor was born in 1949 in Bad Neuenahr, Germany. For more than 140 years and five generations, Gregor's family has been dedicated to floral design and horticulture (the art of gardening). His grandfather was one of the founders of a major flower delivery company. Gregor grew up surrounded by flowers and eventually studied at the Bonn Master's School in Germany. He became a florist (someone who specializes in designing and arranging flowers) himself.

Award-Winning

In 1974 Gregor officially began his career with flowers. He entered his floral designs into various competitions, and in 1978 he won the European Cup, the first time a German had won this international flower competition. From then on, he actively participated in events and won countless awards for his creativity. Gregor didn't have a specific style that he continually relied on. Instead, he focused on creatively challenging himself with natural materials.

Sustainable and Organic

Gregor's interest is in the most natural forms possible: There should not be decorative items or fake flowers that take away from the real beauty of the flowers themselves and lead to further waste. But this does not mean that his works are plain or boring. His designs sometimes include branches, leaves, rocks, moss, and the most sustainable and organic flowers that he can get his hands on. Gregor's arrangements defy gravity, are inspired by cultures around the world, and constantly push the envelope of what is possible. He believes that all the elements of the design should eventually make their way back into the earth.

Teaching

While attending competitions and floral shows, and meeting other flower enthusiasts and beginning floral designers, Gregor knew he needed to share his knowledge and inspiration with others. He started teaching floral design classes in Germany and then expanded further until he began teaching courses around the world. He now speaks more than six languages to help him connect with others. His goal as a teacher is to help people see that designing with flowers should be as natural as the flowers themselves, that anyone can—and should—do it.

Recognition

Beyond his gold medals and championship wins at floral shows, Gregor was awarded the Order of Merit of the Federal Republic of Germany. This recognition is Germany's highest tribute to individuals who uplift society with their achievements in any field. For Gregor, the real reward has been the countless students who have enthusiastically listened to his guidance and have gone out to make the world even more beautiful.

Go Give It a Try!

Gather some flowers (you can purchase these at a grocery store if you can't find any outdoor flowers you are allowed to cut), some branches, leaves, and other natural items. Experiment with creating an arrangement by combining different elements in a vase or jar. Use scissors to adjust the height of the flowers and branches as you try out new possibilities.

Sir Ken Robinson

Education: Teacher
Arts: Advocate

What if kids are born curious and creative, but as they grow up, they aren't encouraged to practice these skills in school and lose the joy of creativity? That is what Sir Ken Robinson, an educator and advocate for arts education, witnessed. And his work has inspired countless educators, schools, and students worldwide.

Life-Threatening Beginnings

Sir Ken was born on March 4, 1950, in Liverpool, England. At the age of four, Sir Ken got polio, a life-threatening virus that can cause someone to not be able to move parts of their body, or even to die. He spent eight months in the hospital battling polio. His dad was a semi-pro soccer player and had thought that his son would follow in his footsteps. But polio had affected Sir Ken's strength and stamina, leaving him in a wheelchair for some time. So, upon returning home, his parents encouraged him to focus on his education.

Education

At first, Sir Ken's parents sent him to a school for students with disabilities. With his determination and his parents' encouragement, he excelled, moving from school to school. When he was sixteen, Sir Ken and some friends wanted to perform a play and worked after school for weeks with a teacher as a director. At one point, the director stepped away from the project and named Sir Ken, a teenager, as the new director. He was shocked but took on the responsibility joyfully. He then decided to get a degree in education, focusing on the arts, especially theater.

Teaching and Researching

Sir Ken began his career in education as the director of the Arts in Schools project, striving to develop arts education all over England and Wales. He worked as a professor of education, researching the importance of creativity in a student's education and for their success in the future.

Global Influence

Sir Ken believed teachers should support their students' individuality by promoting curiosity. He knew that students could discover talents they didn't think they had by trying new things. Sir Ken wanted all schools to focus on awakening the creativity that students are born with. So, he wrote books and gave presentations. He gave three TED Talks, inspiring videos about technology, education, business, science, and creativity. His talks have challenged educators and schools to prioritize creativity and curiosity. At one point, one of his videos was the most-watched TED Talk of all time. In 2003 Sir Ken was knighted by the Queen in recognition of his dedication to the arts. Sir Ken passed away on August 21, 2020. His influence on education was global and continues to impact teachers and students to this day and long into the future.

Go Give It a Try!

Do a creativity workout with a partner. Have your partner draw a crazy shape on a piece of paper. Now it's your turn to take that shape and transform it into a new drawing. Now draw a shape for your partner and have them do the drawing. Work back and forth together, challenging each other's creativity.

Cliff Morrison

Health: Nurse

Even in their darkest, most painful hours, humans crave connection. This is what Cliff Morrison believed as a nurse, and because of him, the care of those diagnosed with AIDS was completely transformed.

Starting Early

Cliff grew up in Live Oaks, Florida. He didn't set out to be a nurse; he was simply looking for a way to help support his family. No one in his family had graduated from high school or attended college, and everyone had to pitch in to contribute to the family's earnings. At the age of twelve, Cliff took a job as a janitor at a local hospital. He mopped floors and took out the trash. After a year of spending time in the hospital and around patients, he asked to take care of patients. Cliff became a hospital orderly, supporting patients with day-to-day tasks and getting them from one place to another. He held this job through his high school graduation.

Change of Plans

Cliff's new plan was to attend nursing school, become the first person in his family to attend college, and then use his earnings to attend medical school to become a doctor. At the time, he had seen men only in the role of doctors and women only as nurses. But he grew to love being a nurse and went on to earn several nursing degrees, including in public health.

Human Contact

Cliff moved to San Francisco and was working in a hospital when the AIDS epidemic began. AIDS is a serious virus that prevents your body from fighting off illness and disease. At the time people were in severe pain, and many were dying. Back then, there were no medicines or treatments that could save infected people's lives. Doctors and nurses who cared for patients with AIDS did their best to avoid contact out of fear of this new illness. Cliff, who had always felt a deep need to care for others at all costs, did what seemed extraordinary at the time: He made those ill with the disease feel like humans. All the patients wanted was to be treated

like people. Cliff reached out to touch and comfort them and refused to wear the space-suit-like protective gear that those around him were wearing. He felt that he knew enough about the disease to know that providing compassionate medical care wasn't going to infect him with the disease.

A New Kind of Care

Because of his efforts to connect with patients, Cliff was asked to be a consultant and help start a new section of the hospital specifically for AIDS patients. Some of the goals of this new care team were to treat the patients with dignity and respect, to allow visitors at almost any time of day, and to redefine the term *family* to allow close friends to visit patients. Touch was also important; those who were sick and dying craved physical contact. Health care facilities around the country later adopted Cliff's methods.

Go Give It a Try!

Patients in hospitals or care facilities crave connection with others. Connection doesn't have to be physical connection. You can create cards that offer encouragement or funny jokes and send them to local hospitals to be distributed by the staff to patients who would appreciate them. Work with a team, club, or your friends to create as many cards as you can.

Ralph Fletcher

Literacy: Author and Writing Advocate

We can get self-conscious about our ideas to the point that we don't share them with others because we fear they aren't good enough or we will be laughed at. Author and writing advocate Ralph Fletcher thinks that to get better at writing, we have to have a place to process, plan, and write out all of our ideas, even if those words are just for us.

Family of Storytellers

Ralph was born on March 17, 1953, in Marshfield, Massachusetts, the oldest of nine kids. He had a big family with many aunts and uncles who would gather and tell rich, beautiful stories. Though Ralph loved listening to his family's tales, his favorite stories involved sports. Ralph wanted to grow up one day to be the center fielder for the Boston Red Sox.

A Magical Job

As Ralph grew up, he loved reading. He thought about the writers of his favorite books and how incredible it was that they sat down and wrote these stories for kids to read. But Ralph never even once considered becoming a writer himself. This job seemed magical and impossible for a kid like him. He had his dreams of baseball to focus on.

Poem for Processing

In high school, Ralph met teachers who encouraged him to do his own writing. And when he met teachers who weren't so encouraging, Ralph wrote in a notebook that he kept all to himself. When he was twenty-one years old, Ralph's brother Bob passed away in a car accident. Ralph had so many emotions, and he didn't know how to process them. He started writing poetry as a way to express all that he was feeling. The loss of his brother became the push and inspiration for Ralph's first novel.

Writer's Notebooks

Ralph loved writing so much that he wanted to share his love with others. He started by working with teachers in New York City, joining them in their classrooms and talking about new ways to excite their students about their own writing. One resource that he was really interested in was the idea of a "writer's notebook." What if there was a place for writers of any age to try out their ideas, make mistakes, and take risks before sharing that writing with other people?

Get Writing

Initially Ralph wrote a book about using a writer's notebook for adults. But the ideas he developed worked well with students, too! Soon, Ralph was sharing his idea for using writer's notebooks with teachers and schools all over the country. He wanted to inspire teachers and their students to see themselves as writers and to encourage students not to seek perfection but to enjoy the act of writing itself. Ralph became a champion of literacy (the ability to read and write) by encouraging other writers and future writers. The boy who never thought he could see himself as a professional writer has written more than twenty books for kids and young adults.

Go Give It a Try!

Begin using your own writer's notebook. You can start by writing poems, short stories about your life, made-up stories, jokes, or any type of writing. Collect your ideas and start thinking about which ones you want to develop further or feel brave enough to share with others.

Joe Hogan
Health: Nurse

What happens when challenges stop you from achieving your goals? Do you give up? Or do you question the way things have always been done? Joe Hogan went with the second choice.

Seeking an Education

Joe earned an associate nursing degree and worked in a hospital. But he wanted more. Joe knew that additional education would make the difference and provide him with more opportunities. He began considering his options for pursuing a bachelor's degree in nursing. But when Joe, who lived in Columbus, Mississippi, researched programs he could apply to, he found that the nearest school was 150 miles (241 km) away.

Very Few Options

It appeared his only option, a co-ed program, was far from home and from the work he was already doing. However, the Mississippi University for Women (MUW) was nearby and had a bachelor's program in nursing. So, in 1979 Joe applied to the school. He was a qualified candidate, a registered nurse, and met all the requirements for admission. But Joe was denied access to the program because he was a man. The university did tell him that he could take classes at the school, but they wouldn't count for credit toward an actual degree.

Challenging the Decision

The whole reason Joe wanted to attend the school was to advance his career; to do that, he needed a degree, so Joe challenged their decision. He took MUW to court for violating his rights as an American citizen. With his first attempt, the court sided with the university. The court said that maintaining MUW's identity as a school for women was significant because it provided excellent opportunities for women. But Joe pushed on, and his case ultimately ended up at the Supreme Court.

The Supreme Court

In 1982 the Supreme Court ruled that MUW's policy was unconstitutional and that Joe and others could attend the publicly funded university. Justice Sandra Day O'Connor was the first woman appointed to the Supreme Court and had the honor of delivering the majority opinion in this case. She supported and explained the court's reasoning for calling MUW's actions unconstitutional. Joe's case ended discrimination based on gender in all publicly funded nursing schools in the entire country. Joe didn't give up when he faced a challenge to his future goals; he kept pushing and questioning and changed access to nursing programs for generations to come.

Go Give It a Try!

Is there a rule at your school that you're frustrated by? First, research why the rule was created by asking adults or older students for their perspective. You may find a good reason for the rule to exist. If not, write an opinion paper to be shared with your principal that includes other students' feedback, why you think the rule should be changed, and how you believe it should be modified. Don't forget to include how you feel this change will benefit the students and staff of the school. Present your opinion to the principal and follow up for feedback on your idea.

LeVar Burton

Literacy: Advocate

The *summer slide* is a term that refers to how kids may lose some of the academic progress they made during the school year because they are not reading during the summer. One of the most excellent solutions to this challenge came from a TV show hosted by actor LeVar Burton. This show catapulted him into classrooms and living rooms around the country and into the role of a literacy (the ability to read and write) advocate.

Potential Futures

LeVar was born on February 16, 1957, in Landstuhl, Germany. He was born on an army base, as his dad was an army photographer and the family was stationed there at the time. LeVar grew up in California, where, at thirteen, he joined a seminary intending to become a priest one day. As a teenager, he realized this wasn't the future he wanted and turned to acting.

Acting Achievements

At the age of nineteen, LeVar broke into the world of acting. He starred in the television miniseries *Roots*. The award-winning miniseries told the story of one African man and his family over generations, during and after slavery in the United States. After that, LeVar had minor acting roles until he was cast as a character on *Star Trek: The Next Generation*. The show was a huge success.

Reading Rainbow

In 1983 LeVar started hosting and producing a show called *Reading Rainbow*. Each episode of the program featured excellent hand-picked picture books that were read out loud for viewers. Other activities and virtual field trips accompanied the book readings, and the show always contained recommendations for kids, narrated by kids. Sometimes, special famous guest readers joined LeVar's hosting. The series went on to win numerous awards, including twelve Emmy awards for LeVar himself.

A Legacy

LeVar promoted reading for an entire generation of kids and made it exciting. *Reading Rainbow* was on TV for more than twenty years. The memorable theme song of the show sparks memories of book read-alouds and LeVar's calming and enthusiastic voice. He has continued to work as an advocate for children's literacy and, in 2017, began a podcast called *LeVar Burton Reads*. With each episode, he reads a short story for adults, some of the very same adults who tuned in to watch him introduce exciting books all those years ago.

Go Give It a Try!

What book have you read recently that you think others would enjoy? Create a recommendation video to be shared with family and friends. Share the book's plot, say who would enjoy it, and reveal some exciting moments you enjoyed. Be careful not to give up the ending or any significant surprises. Share your video with others and ask them to do the same.

Sir Jonathan Elliott Asbridge

Health: Nurse

As we grow, it is important to not forget where we have been and what we have learned. You never know when an experience will inform your future self. This was true for Sir Jonathan Elliott Asbridge, who never forgot where he started.

Resistance

Sir Jonathan, born in 1959 in Cardiff, Wales, had his first taste of nursing when he began work as a cadet with the St. John Ambulance Service in South Wales. He knew at a young age that he wanted to pursue nursing as a career, but his parents were less than excited and strongly fought back. This wasn't the future they wanted for him. Well, Sir Jonathan's story was just beginning.

Many Positions

Sir Jonathan attended nursing school and continued his schooling at a university. With so many possibilities within the nursing profession, Sir Jonathan went from being a staff nurse to a charge nurse in a critical care unit, then an inpatient manager, a general manager, and the director of Clinical Care Services. Eventually he became a director of nursing, then a chief nurse and deputy chief executive. Every step of the way, he was learning alongside other remarkable nurses and gaining firsthand knowledge of life as a nurse. With each new leadership role, Sir Jonathan kept his experience as a practicing nurse central to his decision-making process and the support of his colleagues.

Advocacy and Professionalism

Sir Jonathan was named the inaugural president of the Nursing and Midwifery Council in the United Kingdom. In this role, he took the experiences from his many nursing roles to inform his decisions that would lead to advocacy for nurses and midwives. (A midwife is someone who cares for a mother and her child during the birth of a baby.) Sir Jonathan redesigned and improved how emergency care is provided across the United Kingdom and set goals

for wait times in the A&E (accident and emergency) department. He knew that for patients to receive the best care, the trainings and procedures for nurses had to improve. And nurses needed to be treated as professionals and provided with support that made them feel safe and secure in their work.

Knighthood

Since at least 1860, on the King's or Queen's birthday, individuals are awarded medals, decorations, and appointments. These recognitions celebrate the great works of citizens. On June 17, 2006, Sir Jonathan received such an honor. He was knighted for his dedication to the National Health Service and the advancement of the nursing profession. Thankfully, his family's reluctance about his career choice didn't hold him back from pursuing his dream.

Go Give It a Try!

Contemporary knighthood is an honor and has nothing to do with learning to joust, ride a horse, or shoot an arrow. But have you ever given archery a try? Research local camps or classes that teach the basics of archery. Though this new skill will probably not lead to your future knighthood, it may just become your new favorite activity.

Peter H. Reynolds

Literacy: Author
Arts: Illustrator

When you throw a small pebble into a body of water, a small ripple begins. The ripple expands and expands further from that small beginning point. Peter H. Reynolds may not have thrown a pebble, but his "dot" has engaged people worldwide to consider their own bravery and limitless potential.

Early Publishing Career
Peter was born on March 16, 1961, in Toronto, Canada, along with his identical twin brother, Paul. At the age of three, the family moved to Massachusetts. Here the Reynolds brothers began their publishing career at the age of seven. Peter and his brother used their dad's copy machine to create comic books and newspapers. Peter was constantly doodling and developed his own unique sense of humor.

The Accidental Dot
Peter grew up to be an author and illustrator. Whenever he would introduce himself as an artist, he would hear, "Oh, I can't draw." These responses frustrated Peter because it just meant they hadn't really tried yet. One night in 2001, Peter sat down with his journal and immediately fell asleep. When he woke up an hour later, he realized his permanent marker had bled on the paper and made a large dot. This dot felt special. He signed his name and hung the dot above the fireplace.

The Storied Dot
From Peter's accidental dot, he started writing the book that would one day be called *The Dot*. In this story, a child who questions her drawing abilities meets a teacher who challenges her to be brave and see where a single dot could take her. Peter's book has been translated into numerous languages and inspired a series of books focusing on creativity, bravery, and self-expression.

International Dot Day
In 2009 Terry Shay, a teacher in Iowa, introduced his class to *The Dot* during a one-day celebration of creativity, courage, and collaboration. Their celebration took place on the book's publication anniversary, September 15. Since that day, each September more and more students and their teachers join in on International Dot Day. The day is a celebration around the world, with librarians, teachers, and students from more than 189 countries participating.

His Mission
The ripples continue from that pebble, that initial dot. Peter has gone on to write and illustrate numerous books. He has opened his own bookstore and works alongside his siblings to encourage creativity and learning for everyone. With all of his projects, Peter's mission shines through. He wants to tell stories that matter and dares us to reach for our full potential.

Go Give It a Try!
Pointillism is a technique of filling the page with different colored dots that create an image based on how close they are together or overlap. The most famous pointillism image is *A Sunday on La Grande Jatte*. Use markers to create a pointillism picture made entirely of dots.

Yu "Phillip" Xu
Health: Nurse

When a nurse moves to the United States from another country, there can be challenges, misunderstandings, and frustration from both the patients and the nurse. But how can both parties learn to approach one another with empathy (understanding and sharing the feelings and experiences of others)? That is what Yu "Phillip" Xu strove to explore throughout his life's research.

Lifelong Student

Yu was born in 1961 in Zheng Zhou, China. He went to school in China, studying English and education until he moved to the United States to attend a PhD program for education. In 1996 Yu completed a degree in nursing from a community college in Alabama. And in 1999 he completed a master's degree in public health nursing. He then taught and led nursing programs at several universities. Yu's pursuit of learning took him from studying English to education to nursing, and now to educating future nurses.

Supporting International Nurses

Yu knew firsthand what it was like navigating life and work in the United States as an English language learner. Researching how to support international nurses in the United States became his life's work. He published more than fifty-six research reports and articles on the subject. Yu advocated for the professionalism of international nurses and their excellent knowledge of nursing practices. However, the English language can be challenging and lead to confusion.

Speak for Success

Yu developed a training program in Las Vegas to support international nurses called Speak for Success. In the program, Yu and a speech pathologist worked with nurses to teach them about the uniqueness of the English language and American culture. Jokes or phrases that may make sense or be funny to native English speakers led only to confusion for international nurses. Yu's successes with this program and his research led to his work as a consultant to nursing programs nationally and internationally. He stressed to the medical community that though language was a temporary barrier, the diverse lived experiences of international nurses connected to the ever-diversifying population of the United States.

Recognition

Yu served as president of the Asian American/Pacific Islander Nurses Association. He won awards for excellence in research from universities he worked with. But he saw that his real recognition came from the successful transition of international nurses into the American health system. Yu passed away on July 9, 2013, after battling cancer for years.

Go Give It a Try!

Try learning a new language. Sign up for a course offered at your school or community center. You can look for available apps or technology resources to support your learning. Consider what language you have always been interested in learning and jump in. You have to start somewhere.

Mo Willems

Literacy: Author
Arts: Illustrator

Cartoon animals with speech bubbles have taught countless kids that we all experience a wide range of emotions and that being silly doesn't have to stop when you "grow up." Author and illustrator Mo Willems has had a career that includes television, theater, books, and art exhibits. His illustrated world reminds us of the power of reading, writing, and drawing.

The Peanuts
Mo was born on February 11, 1968, in Des Plaines, Illinois. When he was four, his family moved to New Orleans. Mo loved drawing, and his favorite thing to draw was the characters from Charles Schulz's *Peanuts* cartoons, Charlie Brown and Snoopy. He would dream up his own stories for these characters and create his own cartoons. A five-year-old Mo wrote Charles Schulz a letter containing the line, "Can I have your job when you're dead?"

The Street
Won't you tell me how to get to Sesame Street? Mo knows how; he started working for *Sesame Street* as a writer and animator for nine seasons, earning him six Emmy awards. He later created two animated series and worked as a head writer on another. Mo decided to take a break from television to focus on his writing career.

The Pigeon
In 2003 Mo published his first book, *Don't Let the Pigeon Drive the Bus!* The book became a bestseller, was inducted into the Picture Book Hall of Fame, and won a Caldecott Honor (an award for book illustration). Beyond a pigeon, Mo went on to write books about an elephant and pig duo, a misplaced rabbit, a baguette-obsessed frog, and so many more expressive characters. Mo allows his characters to experience and express a wide range of emotions that make them relatable to kids and adults alike. Remembering the childhood joy he experienced drawing Schulz's cartoons, Mo purposefully designed characters that kids could easily re-create with simple shapes. He wants his readers to dream up new possibilities for his characters and their own silly stories.

The Kennedy Center
The Kennedy Center is the National Cultural Center for the United States, located in Washington, D.C. In 2019 the Center named Mo their first-ever education artist-in-residence. In this role, he developed programming and wrote musical theater productions based on his books. When the COVID-19 pandemic hit the United States in 2020, Mo produced a video series called Lunch Doodles with Mo Willems! He aimed to entertain and engage his audience with drawing, humor, and a glimpse into his world as an author and illustrator.

Go Give It a Try!
Take a look at Mo Willems's characters. Use simple shapes to draw one or many of them in a completely new situation. Create a comic strip, a short book, or an artistic masterpiece. Go ahead, Mo would want you to!

Kwame Alexander
Literacy: Poet and Author

Everyone has different experiences with books during their childhood. Some kids have a few special books they reread over and over again. Others are surrounded by countless piles of books collected over time. And still, some kids don't own a single book. Poet, author, and literacy (the ability to read and write) advocate Kwame Alexander believes in the power of the written word to change the world, working to bring powerful books into all kids' lives.

Surrounded by Books

Kwame was born on August 21, 1968, in New York City and grew up in Virginia. During his childhood, he was surrounded by books because his dad was a writer and publisher and his mom was an English teacher. Reading was an important part of his childhood experience, but Kwame didn't want to read anymore. He wanted to play basketball. It wasn't that he hated reading; he hated being forced to read specific books instead of choosing his own reading material. Young Kwame created his first poem at the age of twelve. When he went to college, he considered a future in medicine. His plans changed when he took a writing class with the famous poet Nikki Giovanni. He was hooked.

Books and Book Festivals

The books that Kwame writes are for all sorts of audiences, including children, young adults, and adults. He writes stories, novels, and poems. Many of Kwame's characters reflect the lived experiences of African Americans, and his poems are responses to his own life and relationships. Frustrated by how national book festivals had few authors of color, Kwame decided to take matters into his own hands. He developed a book festival to reach diverse audiences and feature African American authors. The festival, named Capital Book Fest, started small and then expanded to several cities in the United States and the Caribbean.

Advocacy Work

Poetry can change the world. This is what Kwame believes. He works as an advocate for literacy around the world. Kwame started two organizations, one promoting creative writing and publishing for students. He has helped guide thousands of student authors in the United States, Canada, and the Caribbean to see their potential as writers. Another of Kwame's initiatives focuses on providing literacy support for students and their teachers in Ghana, Africa. He brought twenty other writers and activists to Ghana, where they delivered books, built a library, and offered professional learning opportunities for more than three hundred reading teachers. The team secured scholarship money to provide girls with the opportunity to attend high school.

Many Projects

Beginning with his success as a writer, Kwame's interests and involvement continue to expand. He won several significant awards, including the Newbery Medal, for his best-selling works. Kwame partners with schools and communities as a guest author. He is now producing television programming for kids and adults as well as podcasts, all with a passion for inspiring engagement with the written word.

Go Give It a Try!

As the poet-in-residence for the radio show *Morning Edition*, Kwame would provide the audience prompts to respond to, which he would then combine into poetry. Have your family members respond to one of Kwame's prompts, "Love is . . ." Collect all their responses and connect the lines to form a family poem. Don't forget to contact distant relatives via a call or text.

Dean Vendramin
Education: Teacher

Math can be fun. Math can provide you with opportunities to practice your creativity, problem-solving, and teamwork. This is what teacher Dean Vendramin believes, and he uses creative approaches like video games to make it all happen.

Rooted in Regina

Dean was born on June 10, 1971, in Regina, Canada, where he attended elementary, high school, and even college. As a kid, his parents modeled the importance of helping others and how good it feels when you made a positive difference. Dean realized it was true; helping people brought a sparkle to his eye. And who helps others? Teachers.

Math Teacher

Dean became a high school math and social studies teacher in the same city of the school that had taught him so much as a kid. But he kept thinking he couldn't teach his students the same way he had been taught. Dean knew that in the future, his students would be faced with challenges and opportunities that don't even exist yet. He began to think of new ways to teach and engage his students.

Minecraft

At home, his two sons were playing one of their favorite games, Minecraft. In the game, whole worlds were being built brick by brick, but there was also the potential for so much math learning. Dean created a new way to teach math that focused on real-world challenges while using a virtual format. He gave students assignments to design roller coasters and water parks and re-create famous architecture around the world. Students started using pencil and paper to plan their designs and then transferred their work to the game. While they placed blocks, they were learning math concepts such as slopes, grades, and trusses while flexing their creativity and problem-solving skills. And sometimes, taking the work one step further, they would bring their creations to life using a 3D printer.

Coaching

As a kid, Dean played with several sports teams and knew the power of learning to work as a team. Now a teacher, he decided to coach several different sports for his community, offering students opportunities to enhance their confidence and collaborative efforts: football, baseball, badminton, and weight lifting, as well as several clubs. But his newfound classroom efforts had Dean investigating a new coaching opportunity in eSports. His team would practice multiplayer games that brought them to local and national competitions. The students were learning about leadership, sportsmanship, and digital citizenship.

Recognition

Dean has been recognized as an exceptional teacher for his work with students, receiving awards and fellowship roles. He was named to the Minecraft Global Mentor Program. In 2023 Dean was honored as the recipient of the Prime Minister's Award for Excellence in Science, Technology, Engineering, and Math.

Go Give It a Try!

Design a roller coaster. Begin by planning your roller coaster on paper. Is this a wild thrill ride or a calmer traditional roller coaster for families? Then, build your roller coaster using a digital program, paper, or found objects around the home.

Kurt Russell
Education: Teacher

Hope is a desire for something to happen. Hope involves trust in the future. So, when National Teacher of the Year Kurt Russell says, "I still have hope," it means something special. These four simple words reveal the truth that a situation might be complicated or frustrating, but you can still have trust in what could happen next.

The Three Wise Men

Kurt was born on October 21, 1971, in Oberlin, Ohio. As a kid, Kurt visited family in Alabama, where his parents were from. In the houses of family members, he saw paintings of Jesus, President John F. Kennedy, and Martin Luther King Jr. He had so many questions about these three men, prompting his love for learning. Kurt's questions were met with stories from his mom about her experiences with segregation (the separation of Black and white people) and the civil rights movement in Alabama.

Seen and Valued

In kindergarten, Kurt's teacher Francine Toss further ignited his passion for learning. She read the class a book about Martin Luther King Jr. that made Kurt feel seen and valued. In the eighth grade, Kurt had his first Black male teacher, Larry Thomas, who taught math. In Thomas, Kurt saw someone who looked like him in front of a class full of engaged students. Kurt saw how teachers have the power to support and motivate others. At that moment, he made a decision: He would one day be a teacher who would inspire and challenge his own students.

The Dream Job

Kurt became a history teacher in the same school he was a student in: Oberlin High School. He called it his dream job. He began teaching general history classes and then designed his own courses about African American history, Black music, and race, gender, and oppression. His goal for each class was to set a safe, inclusive environment for exploring experiences and stories while facing uncomfortable topics. Kurt wanted his students to feel seen, heard, and valued, just as Francine Toss had done for him as a kindergartener.

Coach

Beyond his classroom, Kurt became the head coach of the Oberlin Boys Varsity Basketball team. He viewed his role as an extension of the classroom. Through the relationships built on and off the court, he encouraged the boys he worked with to be resilient and confident. His players had to learn to work together while processing both success and hardship.

National Teacher of the Year

In 2022 Kurt was first named the Ohio Teacher of the Year and then selected as National Teacher of the Year. In this new role, Kurt met with teachers, leaders, families, and students across the country to advocate for opportunities for students and highlight the need for more teachers of color to join the profession. When asked about the current state of education, Kurt responded, "I still have hope." He has hope in educators across the country who provide love and normalcy when the world feels unkind. And he has hope in the inspiring students who will create a better world into the future.

Go Give It a Try!

Kurt has hope in students, teachers, and for the future of education. What is one thing you are hopeful about? Make a poster for your room or a sign for your locker with your hopeful statement. This visual will help remind you to focus forward even when you feel challenged.

Daniel Vijayaraj
Health: Nurse

A life experience can change everything. We may witness an act of kindness that inspires our own acts of selflessness many years down the road, and that was true for a young Daniel Vijayaraj.

Early Experience

Daniel is originally from the Keeladi village in India. As a child, his mom had to have a major surgery. Daniel stayed by her side in the hospital through-out her recovery. During their time in the hospital, Daniel noticed that the nurses who took care of his mom were gentle and respectful of her needs. They showed great patience with both Daniel and his mom. A child himself, he thought about how the nurses treated his mom as if she were their child in need of care and reassurance.

The Spark

While his mom continued to recover from her surgery, the nursing staff taught Daniel how to clean wounds. His mom required medicine, and the nurses taught Daniel how and when to give her the medicine she needed. This was the spark. Learning how to care for someone else when they needed it most—and in this case, someone who had cared for him so thoughtfully since he was born—prompted Daniel to pursue a nursing career.

Nursing as a Career

In 2001 Daniel started working as a nurse in England at South Tees NHS (National Health System) Trust. Over time, he continued to advance his career, learn-ing about different nursing specialties and taking on new roles. One of those roles was to serve as a men-tor to young nursing students. His mission was to offer the same care, explanations, and patience the nurses had provided him as a child when his mom was in the hospital.

Recognition

In 2022 Daniel was honored with the Nightingale Award from the South Tees NHS Trust. The award recognizes nurses who have gone the extra mile regarding patient care. Florence Nightingale, the award's namesake, was from England and the founder of modern nursing who elevated the role of nurses by focusing on patient care. Notably, Daniel's nomination came from several patients who remarked on the exceptional care they received from him. Daniel, the first nurse from India to receive this prestigious award, found the whole experience rather humbling. He viewed his recognition as a challenge to further increase his dedication to his profession and the mentorship he provides to nursing students.

Go Give It a Try!

Have you ever considered being a positive mentor for younger kids at your school or in your community? Research mentorship programs available to you or talk with a school principal about setting up a program. Consider the focus of your mentorship program and what you would like to accomplish. You could read alongside younger students, teach a specific skill, or play games with them. The key is to form a connection through communication and meet with them regularly to build a positive relationship.

Carlos Acosta

Arts: Dancer

The word *ballet* often prompts images of pink tutus, satin shoes, and ribbons. But what about a strong Cuban man who started with very little and then went on to dance across stages worldwide? Carlos Acosta takes the stage.

Incredibly Energetic

Carlos was born on June 2, 1973, in Havana, Cuba. The youngest of eleven kids, Carlos's family had so little money that he grew up without toys and didn't have a birthday cake until he turned twenty-three years old. His dad noticed that his youngest child was incredibly energetic and worried that his energy would get him into trouble, so he enrolled him at the National Ballet School of Cuba. Carlos's dad hoped the school would teach him discipline, but never would he imagine where this decision would take his son.

Gold Medal Status

Carlos excelled in his dance studies. In 1990 he won the Gold Medal at the Prix de Lausanne, an international ballet competition for young dancers fifteen to eighteen years old. For those who participate in this unique competition, there are exciting possibilities. And, for students like Carlos, who won a Gold Medal, the world is open to them. At eighteen, he became the youngest-ever principal dancer with the English National Ballet in London.

Choreography

The Houston Ballet was his home for several years, where he further developed as a dancer. But it was with London's Royal Ballet that Carlos continued to flourish as a dancer and choreographed his own ballet for the company. When someone choreographs a dance, they design the movements the dancers make. Carlos even proudly brought the ballet company to his hometown of Havana for the very first time.

Tocororo

Carlos continued dancing for years as an international guest artist, joining ballet companies around the world. In 2003 he premiered a ballet he choreographed based on his life called *Tocororo*. The ballet opened in Havana and later broke box office records when it was performed in London. Carlos established his own dance company in Havana called Acosta Danza. He tours the world with his dancers, directing and performing alongside them. Carlos hopes that with his dance company, he can further share the vibrant culture of Cuba with the world.

Go Give It a Try!

There are countless proven benefits for those who learn ballet, including flexibility, strength, and balance. Search for ballet stretching routines online and begin to feel the benefits of this dance form. Are you enjoying yourself? Investigate local ballet classes.

Stephen Wiltshire
Arts: Visual Artist

Sometimes, all we need is a champion to notice us and celebrate our abilities beyond our current circumstances. Stephen Wiltshire began his life without communication until he picked up a pencil and began drawing.

Paper and Pencil

Stephen was born on April 24, 1974, in London to his two parents who were originally from the West Indies. At the age of three, Stephen was diagnosed as autistic. He didn't speak or communicate with his family or others in his life. After he enrolled in school, the teachers noticed that the only activity Stephen was interested in was drawing. He would draw animals, buses, and buildings, all with incredible detail. To prompt Stephen to speak, his teachers would make him ask for access to art supplies. His first words were *paper* and *pencil*. It wasn't until the age of nine that Stephen could fully speak.

Taking Notice

The school was buzzing with enthusiasm about Stephen's work, especially the sketches he created of significant London buildings. One of Stephen's teachers became his champion, accompanying him to art exhibits, entering his work in competitions, and going on field trips so that he could draw. Now, other people started to notice his beautifully detailed work, and the media (including newspapers and television) started featuring his art. When Stephen was eight, he sold his first artwork to the British prime minister. His drawing of Salisbury Cathedral, a famous cathedral in England, brought him even more attention.

Skyline Sketches

Stephen was able to create highly detailed drawings of famous buildings and skylines. But it was the character of the building he captured with his line work that fascinated his viewers. Soon, Stephen was invited to draw cities across the globe, impressing everyone with his ability. During a visit to Hong Kong, Stephen went up in a helicopter to view the city from above. The ride was only twenty minutes long, but when he touched back down to the ground, he started on a drawing that would become more than thirty-two feet (10 m) long. He could recall the tiniest detail and include it in his massive drawing.

Global Personality

Stephen's photographic memory (the ability to remember things exactly as they are seen or read) and the ability to draw what he had seen sent him to Australia, Mexico, China, Rome, New York, and more. But cityscapes aren't the only subject that Stephen draws. He creates more drawings of people within a year than buildings. He fills his private sketchbooks with caricatures of his close friends and celebrities. In 2006 Stephen was named by Queen Elizabeth II as a Member of the Order of the British Empire for his remarkable dedication and service to the art world. Later that year, he opened his own art gallery and studio, welcoming visitors by appointment. This artist, who couldn't fully communicate through spoken word until he was nine, was now an art phenomenon around the world.

Go Give It a Try!

Drawing from memory is an excellent way to boost your awareness skills, regardless of your drawing ability. Look at your living room for three minutes. Look for the details you don't always notice. Then go into the other room and draw everything you can remember. When you are done, head back to the living room to see how well you captured this space.

Miguel Cardona
Education: Teacher

What happens when someone doesn't believe you can amount to much? Sometimes, their disbelief in you makes you more driven to do your best and redefine your potential. Miguel Cardona, a child growing up in public housing who didn't even learn English until kindergarten, never gave up. His drive has taken him to Washington, D.C., where he relentlessly advocates for students and teachers.

Puerto Rican Proud

Miguel was born on July 11, 1975, in Meriden, Connecticut. The son of two Puerto Rican parents, Miguel grew up in a public housing community, speaking Spanish as his first language. He only started learning English when he enrolled in kindergarten. His family celebrated their heritage through music. Miguel learned to play the bongo drums and played alongside his brother and dad at community events, including the town's Puerto Rican festival.

More Than Capable

When Miguel was in school, he often felt that people had lower expectations for what he could achieve. This only made him even more hungry to prove them wrong, to show everyone what he was capable of. In high school, Miguel studied at a technical school focusing on car repair while taking college preparatory classes. When it was time to apply to college, he started down a path in art education because of the influence of his incredible art teacher. But Miguel ultimately settled on elementary education. He saw the promise and the potential in their young eyes and knew he wanted to be their champion.

Classroom Experience

Miguel started his education career in a fourth-grade classroom in the same school district he attended as a child. At twenty-eight, he became the youngest principal in the state's history, leading an elementary school with exceptional programming for preschoolers, bilingual students, and students with sensory needs. In 2012 Miguel received the National Distinguished Principal Award for the state of Connecticut. After ten years in this role, he became the district's assistant superintendent.

Tour Guide

Remembering his roots and experiences as an English language learner, as assistant superintendent, Miguel would take every new hire on a tour of the district. He wanted these new educators to see the diverse communities they were serving, to give them an understanding that all of these students were now their students. He was committed to making a strong public education available for all students and took this belief to the state level as the commissioner for education in Connecticut.

U.S. Secretary of Education

On March 2, 2021, Miguel was named the twelfth U.S. Secretary of Education. In this new role, he dreamed of possibilities to positively impact the more than sixty-five million students in the United States. He wanted them to receive an excellent education that valued who they were as individual learners and with teachers who knew they were supported by a leader who was also an educator.

Go Give It a Try!

There are parts of your community you have never visited and maybe even some great surprises to discover. Make a map of your local community, including areas of interest you know about. Take the map as you walk or drive around your neighborhood with an adult, discovering new locations. Add your new sites to your map to share later with others.

Corey Bulman
Education: Teacher

If you could have one superhero power, what would it be? Did you happen to consider curiosity? For Corey Bulman, he believes his superpower, curiousness, has driven him to keep learning and growing throughout his life. It led him to teaching, where he empowers his students to question, listen, and learn.

Early Struggles

Corey was born on August 4, 1975, in Wisconsin. He wasn't the best of students in elementary school, Corey struggled with traditional learning in reading and math. But he had teachers who believed in him and his potential. Though he may have been challenged in class, he had a skill all his own, one that may not have come naturally to his classmates. He was curious.

Trivia Time

As a kid, a trivia game for adults became super popular. Corey sat reading each card and memorizing the answers. He would later challenge adults to play the game. At first, Corey questioned if learning the answers from the cards was a form of cheating until he realized he was actually learning from the game. Corey was interested in learning everything and anything he could. And here was a way for him to do just that.

New Skills

Corey's high school art teacher and theater director provided Corey with opportunities to challenge his curiosity and develop new skills. At the University of Minnesota, Corey questioned whether to pursue being a lawyer or become a teacher. Then, he stopped and asked himself, "Which role would have the greater impact on others?" He knew the answer. Corey became a high school English teacher in Minnesota.

Role Model

In his classroom, Corey provides students with opportunities to study literature and poetry. But each day, he models curiosity for them, too. He gives students the chance to share about their lives with him and one another. Corey knows that all his students, especially the boys he works with, need to see a role model who is empathetic (understanding and sharing the feelings and experiences of others), curious, and gracious. Corey listens with empathy to his students' stories of losing a loved one, a feeling he personally knows too well, having lost his son to cancer. When students question what they will do next after graduation, he remembers being where they are, too. He doesn't need to have all the correct answers anymore. There are no trivia cards to memorize in these situations, but he now knows the power of stopping and intentionally listening.

Five Minutes

Corey steps aside at the end of each school year, saying that he has shared as much as he can with his students. It is now their turn to share. Each student prepares a five-minute presentation on any topic that matters to them. The students share presentations on balloon animals, dance, music, or life without a beloved family member. The other students listen with empathy and amazement. Corey's curiosity is now contagious. In 2017, a long way from his early elementary years, he was recognized as Minnesota's Teacher of the Year.

Go Give It a Try!

Create your own trivia game to share with your family and friends. Focus on topics you know well or that you want to better understand. Consider whether you will use multiple-choice questions or statements asking players to consider whether the information is true or false. Develop rules for your game and enough questions for everyone to join in the fun.

Babak Mashhadi Ebrahim
Education: Teacher

Equity is different from equality. Equality means everyone receives the same thing, whereas equity recognizes that not all people start from the same place and need special adjustments to fix imbalances. Babak Mashhadi Ebrahim uprooted his whole life for equity and continues to work with his students, using equity as his guide.

A Life-Changing Decision

Babak immigrated to the United Kingdom from Iran in 2000. The move wasn't an easy decision, and it would change not only his life but also the lives of his family members. Babak, the father of two girls, wanted to provide his daughters with more opportunities. In the United Kingdom, his daughters could experience more opportunities than in their home country, which limited women's rights and access to education.

Access for Girls

Babak began work as a math and computer science teacher. With his focus on equity-driven teaching, Babak made a disheartening discovery. Though the United Kingdom was a place where he knew girls and women could thrive and be successful, in his classroom, girls were underrepresented. Those who were enrolled participated less than their male classmates and lacked confidence. Babak decided he needed to be the solution by offering girls an opportunity to thrive.

Cyber Girls

Babak formed his school's first Cyber Girls team. The team of girls would work together to learn about cybersecurity practices and put their learning to the test during competitions. In the United Kingdom, the National Cyber Security Centre hosts a CyberFirst competition. Babak signed up the team. In 2002 the team of girls won first place; in 2023 they reached the finals. But there was more than just the competitions. In his classes, Babak featured women speakers, offered coding competitions, and organized technology showcases. The goal was to encourage more girls to consider a future in technology.

Coaching

Babak noticed an imbalance of equal access for girls compared with boys in other areas. His daughters showed an interest in soccer, leading him to coach his school's girls' soccer team. Babak wanted to ensure that all opportunities available for his male students were accessible to his female students and, especially, his daughters. In Babak's heart, he knew that all children deserved a chance to succeed. And he was going to be part of the solution.

Pandemic and Recognition

During the COVID-19 pandemic, Babak wanted all students to have access to technological learning. He started after-school clubs, workshops, and collaborations with businesses. And, in 2023 Babak was named one of fifty finalists for the Global Teacher Prize, the winner of which receives $1 million.

Go Give It a Try!

There are downloadable cybersecurity games that are suitable for adults and students alike. With the help of an adult, locate one of these games as you develop and apply a basic understanding of defense strategies.

EDUCATION

Peter Tabichi

Education: Teacher

Going to school is something that a lot of people take for granted. But countless kids around the world have little access to teachers, technology, and transportation to school. Peter Tabichi knows this truth all too well, but this empowering teacher will stop at nothing to provide a world-class education for his students.

Access to Education

Peter was born in 1982 in a rural part of Kenya, Africa. He grew up as one of eight kids in a family of teachers. His dad and several of his cousins were teachers. Peter's dad worked diligently to provide his children with the best education they could access, but that didn't mean it was easy. Peter had to walk more than four miles (6.5 km) every day to school. There he saw teachers' power to inspire students to reach for their potential.

Simplicity and Justice

Peter became a Franciscan friar, which is a specific role within the Catholic Church where men dedicate themselves to a life of poverty centered on simplicity, justice, and the care of others. Peter carries these values wherever he goes, especially in his classroom. He began teaching math and science in a rural school community in the Great Rift Valley in Kenya. The community is impacted by famine (extreme lack of food), drought (extreme dryness), and community conflict. Many of his students come from different tribes and villages. Peter started a peace club, where students who would have typically gotten involved in fights engaged instead in tree planting, sports, and activities that prompted them to work together and learn about one another.

Beyond the Classroom Walls

The school where Peter had been teaching had one desktop computer, no access to Wi-Fi, no kitchen, and only one teacher for every fifty-eight students. For Peter, being an educator isn't just about the walls of his classroom. He works with community members, teaching them about drought-resistant plants and the potential of renewable energy (energy that comes from a source that will not run out). Students in his classroom engaged in a project where they grew local plants to generate power. The project won the students a national award and invitations to travel around the world to share their research findings.

Good in the World

Peter hopes that students will believe in their potential. They are. In just a couple of years, with his support, the number of students attending university doubled. For Peter, his work has never been about himself. It has always been about the good he put out into the world. But people did take notice. In 2019, out of ten thousand nominations, Peter received the Global Teacher Prize, an international recognition of teachers. He was awarded $1 million, a staggering amount of money for an individual who had always given 80 percent of his teacher's salary back to his community. With his winnings, Peter hoped to bring Wi-Fi, a modern computer lab, and water to his students.

Go Give It a Try!

Research which drought-tolerant plants are native to your community. These plants can offer access to food, add beauty to your space, and provide habitats for local wildlife. Work with an adult to plan a way to start these plants in a yard or container. You will need less water to help these plants thrive.

Luke Haynes
Arts: Quilter

Wrapping blankets and sheets over the backs of chairs and propped-up pillows, a young Luke Haynes created forts in his living room. These forts and the safety and warmth they created prompted him to explore a future as an architect, but ultimately he became a quilter.

Temporary

Luke was born on September 28, 1982. His parents divorced when he was young, and he spent his childhood moving from state to state. He lived in seven southern U.S. states. Luke was curious, built with plastic bricks whenever he could, and pulled together family blankets for making forts. The homes they lived in always seemed so temporary, which prompted Luke to consider what safe, stable homes could look like and to pursue a future as an architect.

Architecture School

Architecture school seemed like the right fit for Luke. Through his studies, he was investigating how a building could provide comfort and stability. But, he realized that maybe there was a better way to create works that addressed what he was looking for. In 2002 Luke made his first quilt, and there was no going back.

Warmth

Luke taught himself how to sew. His architectural learning supported his new adventures with fabrics, leading him to experiment and manipulate his material. This art form that so easily brings to mind images of grandmothers and warmth on chilly nights spoke to Luke. He understood that quilts were often lovingly created for survival and warmth. Just as he did with architecture, quilting seemed like a way that he could create safe spaces.

Thrift Stores

Luke now finds himself revisiting the thrift stores like those he spent time in as a kid. But this time, it wasn't to find clothing for himself but to find materials for his quilts. He selects used clothes and materials to reference his past and spark memories for others through his quilts. When designing his quilts, Luke follows traditional patterns with a twist. Other times, his artwork features stylized portraits, french fries, balloon animals, and even Croc shoes.

Affirmation Quilts

Luke works with his wife, Nicole, on anonymous (without a name) quilting projects. Luke creates a usable quilt that includes a hand-painted note of affirmation from Nicole. Then, the two leave the quilt somewhere to be discovered, kept, and used by anyone who needs it. Luke and Nicole don't do this project to get attention; their names aren't even attached to the quilt. They hope that their work is found by someone who could benefit from the quilt's warmth and safety.

Go Give It a Try!

Have you ever tried sewing? Locate a thread, needles, fabric, and a pair of scissors. After threading the needle and tying a knot at the end of the string opposite the needle, practice a running stitch through a piece of fabric. Push the needle through, leaving small lines of thread that continuously go under the fabric and then over the fabric. You should create what looks like a dotted line. Once you get the hang of it, research simple sewing projects.

Candido Crespo
Education: Teacher
Arts: Visual Artist

Changes to our daily routines and expectations can prove challenging. But what if these changes spark a sense of creativity that becomes contagious? That is what happened to Candido Crespo as he went from being an artist and teacher to being an artist, teacher, and dad who inspires other male role models to get creative.

Choices

Candido was born on August 26, 1984, in East Meadow, New York. Like so many kids, Candido was asked repeatedly what he wanted to do with his future. In middle school, he wrestled with the idea that he wanted to be either an art teacher or a veterinarian. Candido couldn't make up his mind and then realized he didn't have to decide just yet. During high school, Candido faced some challenges requiring teachers to come alongside and help him. These caring teachers confirmed that he wanted to be a teacher and to pay it forward by supporting his future students through their challenges.

Curiosity and Love

Right after college, Candido was hired into his dream job, teaching high school art classes to predominately Latinx and Black students. Since then, he has taught intermediate, middle school, and elementary students. Even with new classes and students of different ages, the one thing that didn't change was Candido's teaching style, which centers on curiosity and love. Though he was providing students with artistic experiences, his goal wasn't to develop a ton of working artists but to give students the confidence to try new things, explore possibilities, and face challenges with the knowledge that he was on their side.

Art Making and Podcasting

While teaching in the classroom, Candido shares his art with his students. He wants them to see his creative process and the skills he has developed, that the creation of a work of art is not something just in history books. He creates paintings, drawings, digital images, and whatever inspires his creativity. Candido hosted a podcast called the *Everyday Art Room*; the audience was other art teachers who were learning alongside him as he engaged with guest artists and educators each week.

CreativDAD

In 2018 Candido became a dad, and he was nervous that he would lose his time to be creative and make art, an important part of his identity and well-being. As soon as his son could hold art materials, the two, father and son, would sit together and spend time being creative. Candido realized that his new art-making partnership with his son could inspire fathers and male guardians to sit and be creative alongside the children in their lives. Candido offers workshops and presentations with simple directions, materials, and a whole lot of space for men and their kids to be creative. As soon as Candido's son was old enough to attend the workshops, he was introduced to the families in attendance as the coteacher.

Go Give It a Try!

Consider which male role model in your life you would like to sit down and be creative with, using one of Candido's drawing prompts. Together, draw what an epic battle between a monster and a robot would look like.

Jermar Rountree

Education: Teacher

Oh, it's as easy as riding a bike! Have you ever heard someone say this statement to describe an activity? But what if you never learned how to ride a bike? Physical education teacher Jermar Rountree decided to change his students' lives with this very realization.

Human Connection

Jermar was born on October 6, 1984, in Waterbury, Connecticut. As a kid, Jermar was never really sure how long he would be at at any elementary school because he switched schools often. He quickly learned how to be adaptable, how to make friends, and the power of making people laugh. The strong relationships he built at each school taught him the power of human connection and how to cope with difficult challenges.

Correction Officer

In college, Jermar made a commitment with his roommate to become a correction officer, undergoing rigorous training. All the while, he felt a strong pull toward teaching. Jermar started work as a correction officer when, one day, he came upon a nineteen-year-old who was in and out of the facility. This young man had always struggled with reading and couldn't even read a letter his parents had sent him. Jermar read it to him, and it said that his parents could no longer support him based on his poor decisions. The letter was heartbreaking for the young man and confirmed what Jermar knew all along: Becoming a teacher was his calling. He wanted to help young people form a strong foundation at an early age, set them up to be successful, and help them even when others seemed to have given up on them.

The Bikes

Jermar started teaching at a school in Washington, D.C., where he taught physical education to pre-K through eighth-grade students. One day, he realized that most of his students, living in a city environment, had never learned to ride a bike. Jermar worked with community partners and bought twenty-four bikes for his students to use. Not only did he teach them about balance and road safety, but he continually did emotional and mental check-ins to see how they were feeling throughout their learning. It can be hard to learn something new, and he wanted to offer them the support they needed to be successful.

Freedom

With their new bikes, the students saw their city, Washington, D.C., like they had never seen it before. Learning how to ride a bike with Jermar had offered them new freedom to ride past the National Zoo, the White House, and national monuments. Who knows where Jermar's students will go next because of the confidence and human connection he provided them?

Recognition

That kid who had formed relationships at each new elementary school he attended was now focused on building relationships with his students and their families. And in 2023 Jermar was named the District of Columbia Teacher of the Year. He was later recognized as one of five 2023 National Teacher of the Year finalists.

Go Give It a Try!

How often do you do an emotional and mental check-in with yourself when you are learning something new? When you are learning something new, stop, take a breath, and check in with yourself. Are you proud of your work? Are you feeling energized or frustrated? Do you feel lost and confused? Once you understand where you are emotionally, consider what support you need to keep the new learning going.

Eddie Woo

Education: Teacher

Empathy can be defined as understanding and sharing the feelings and experiences of others. When we empathize with others, we can think of ways to help them in times of need. That happened with math teacher Eddie Woo, who made decisions from a place of empathy that would take his impact beyond the four walls of his classroom and out into the world.

Opportunities

Eddie was born in 1985 in New South Wales, Australia. Earlier, his parents had come to Australia from Malaysia, seeking better education opportunities for their children. However, as a child, Eddie was bullied by other students because of his Asian heritage. In school, Eddie worked hard and excelled in his studies, especially math. With his exceptional grades and intelligence, Eddie could have gone on to almost any career; he chose teaching and never looked back.

Teaching with Empathy

Eddie became a math teacher. Throughout his studies, Eddie identified that math was a challenge to sometimes understand. His journey to grasp difficult mathematical concepts allowed him to develop empathy for his students who may have found math difficult. This empathy led him to teach with enthusiasm and creativity. In 2012 one of Eddie's students was battling cancer and missing a lot of school. This hit Eddie hard—his own family had been deeply affected by cancer when he was in high school. Eddie began recording his math classes for the student, who could take their time watching the videos to grasp concepts they would have missed. The videos were engaging and helpful, and Eddie decided to post them on YouTube, hoping they would help other students with challenging math concepts.

WooTube

His videos became known as WooTube, and before long, he had more than one hundred thousand subscribers and millions of views of his virtual math lessons. Students found Eddie's videos easy to follow, and with the virtual format they could pause and replay the lessons over and over until they further understood the content. Eddie's presence on the screen prompted his involvement in several television programs in Australia, including hosting the program *Teenage Boss*. In this show, teenagers were given control of their family's finances for a month, making all decisions about how money was spent and saved while learning lessons about responsibility and planning.

Recognition

Eddie has been recognized for his work with several awards and recognitions. He won the Australia's Local Hero Award, he gave the Australia Day address (the first classroom teacher ever to do so) in New South Wales, and in 2018 he was named a top ten finalist for the Global Teacher Prize. Through all the recognition, Eddie continues to lead from the classroom with empathy and enthusiasm.

Go Give It a Try!

Eddie hosted a show about teenagers learning about finances. Have a family discussion about the grocery store and how much money your family tries to spend each week on food. Work with an adult to set a budget for food for a week. Visit the grocery store with an adult and decide what to buy and what not to buy to stick to your goal amount.

Will Pooley

Health: Nurse

To fight a deadly illness is one thing. To then contract this fatal illness brings about a whole other set of challenges. Fighting your way back to health and then returning to your mission of saving others takes a brave hero. This is the story of Will Pooley.

Part of the Solution

Will was born in Suffolk, United Kingdom. In 2013 he qualified as a nurse. Africa had always been on Will's mind as a place he had wanted to work. So, in 2014 he traveled to Sierra Leone to work with a non-profit. Will heard about how an Ebola virus outbreak was out of control, especially in one Sierra Leone hospital unit. He knew he needed to be part of the solution: the care the patients were receiving. He made up his mind and began the journey that would change everything.

Fight Against Ebola

Ebola is a rare but often fatal disease that causes high fevers and bleeding inside the body. At the Ebola treatment center where Will worked, most patients died from the horrible disease, including several of his fellow nurses. The center had difficulty getting enough staff to care for the infected patients, meaning his patients were frequently left alone in the evenings. Often, Will would come to work in the morning to find that patients he had cared for had passed away during the night. He continued to do the best he could with the resources he had, prompting him to improvise, but what they needed most were more nurses.

Infection

On a Friday, six weeks after starting at the hospital, Will woke up with a sudden fever. After testing, it was confirmed that he had contracted Ebola. To the best of his memory, Will had always worn his personal protection equipment and was incredibly careful with his patients. But one time he cared for a small baby who had tested negative after the mother had died. Later, the baby tested positive. Will's positive diagnosis prompted him to be flown out of the country and back to England in an isolation tent set up in the back of a transporter airplane.

Care

In England, Will was scared; he knew firsthand what this virus had done to people he had cared for and worked alongside. He received the best care in the world for his Ebola infection, including experimental medicine. Only after his health improved did Will begin to wrestle with his own ability to access remarkable care versus what his patients could acquire in Sierra Leone. It was this truth that sent him back to Africa, where he would continue to fight the fatal disease.

Emotional Connection

At the age of thirty, a year after his airlift out of Sierra Leone, Will began work at the very same hospital in London that saved his life after he contracted Ebola. He felt an emotional connection to the hospital and knew that in this place he could continue caring for patients, giving back what he had been given—a new chance at life.

Go Give It a Try!

Africa is a huge continent with more than fifty diverse countries. Spend some time researching this amazing continent to find out what the most commonly spoken language is. Or what is the most populous country? What other countries besides Egypt have pyramids? And what unique building material is used in Tunisia for good luck? What other unique facts can you learn about this richly diverse continent?

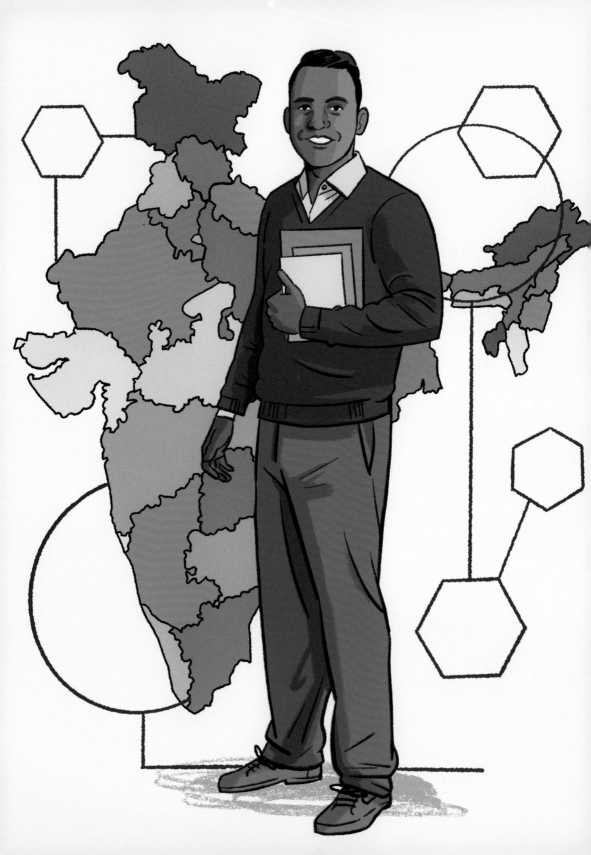

Ranjitsinh Disale

Education: Teacher

How does someone become a change maker? They have awareness, advocate, and find solutions to obstacles. For teacher Ranjitsinh Disale, becoming a change maker meant changing his career aspirations, learning a new language, challenging the poor treatment of girls, and providing his students with opportunities beyond their available resources.

A Change of Plans

Ranjitsinh was born on August 5, 1988, in Paritewadi, India. He grew up in Maharashtra, dreaming of becoming an IT (information technology) engineer. Decisions and plans were made that resulted in Ranjitsinh enrolling in engineering college. But it wasn't all he thought it would be, and he was left wondering, "What do I do now?" His dad suggested that he investigate becoming a teacher. Ranjitsinh resisted at first, but after only a few days in a teacher training program, he realized that teachers are the world's change makers. And he wanted to be part of that movement.

Next to the Cattle Shed

In 2009 Ranjitsinh had his first teaching position at the Zilla Parishad Primary School. The building needed repairs and was located between a cattle shed and a storeroom. Most of the girls who attended the school were from local tribal communities, where teenage marriage was common and a girl's education wasn't seen as a priority. Girls' attendance at the school would sometimes hit 2 percent. Ranjitsinh saw himself as part of the solution. He worked to fix up the school, advocated for all his students to attend, and did everything in his power to support his students' learning.

Solution Seeking

One obstacle for Ranjitsinh is that he didn't speak the primary language of his students, Kannada. The textbooks available to his students weren't even written in their language. He began learning Kannada to communicate and connect with his students and their community, and translate their readings. Ranjitsinh saw that their books were limited in their information and didn't offer his students a chance for individual learning. So, he redesigned them, adding a QR code into every book. Now, he could provide his students personalized learning opportunities with audio recordings, video lectures, and further readings they could access anywhere. This strategy was so successful that the practice was soon adopted by national organizations in India and brought to schools nationwide.

Successes

In 2016 his school was named the best school in its district. The attendance of Ranjitsinh's students rose to a point where 100 percent of the girls were attending school, and teenage marriage had become nonexistent in the village. One of his female students went on to graduate from university, an accomplishment that seemed near impossible before Ranjitsinh became their teacher. In 2016 the government of India named him the Innovative Researcher of the Year. In 2020 Ranjitsinh won the Global Teacher Prize, an award that comes with a $1 million prize. He decided to take half of this award money and split it up among the nine other finalists. He believed that with these funds, these nine educators could further their incredible work for students and ultimately change the world.

Go Give It a Try!

Is a friend's or a relative's birthday coming up? Record a video of yourself offering a birthday greeting. Use a QR code generator, available for free online, to create a QR code that links to your video message. Combine the virtual and the physical by printing the code and adding it to a card you send in the mail.

Curtis Oland
Arts: Fashion Designer

How often do you consider your clothing and where the design and the materials come from? And what about when you are done wearing them? Where do those pieces of clothing go next? These are the thoughtful considerations that fashion designer Curtis Oland puts into the design of his theatrical clothing pieces as he pulls inspiration from his indigenous (native) heritage.

Magic and Imagination

Curtis was born in 1989 and grew up in the Okanagan Valley of British Columbia, Canada. His mother's background is indigenous, of the Lil'wat Nation, and his dad's heritage is Scottish. The family chose to live relatively off-grid. There was no cable, no Nintendo, no white bread. But there was magic and imagination. The family loved Halloween, and young Curtis saw this as a time to create new characters and explore new identities.

Intro to Fashion

Curtis went on to enroll in college, where he studied sculpture. In his second year at school, he was introduced to fashion. He became interested in the history of costume design and fibers. He learned about new designers who combined fashion, sculpture, and expression. Curtis knew that he needed to be part of this world. He enrolled in fashion design school.

Cultural Inspiration

In his designs, Curtis draws inspiration from his rich cultural heritage and the mountainous landscape of his home. He thoughtfully uses raw natural materials like wool, silk, linen, organic cotton, and deer and elk skins, the traditional materials of the Lil'wat people. Honoring the natural strength of the materials, Curtis often uses the raw edges of the animal skins that others would throw away and finds beauty in the frayed edges of fabrics that other designers would clean up. Curtis wants his designs to cause us to consider how what we wear connects us

spiritually, to one another, and to the land. In 2016 Curtis won the Emerging Menswear Designer Award at Toronto Men's Fashion Week, further propelling his unique work into conversations about contemporary fashion.

Cultural Stereotypes

Working in London, Curtis became aware that others had stereotypes and preconceived ideas of what it meant to be an indigenous person. He worked alongside other indigenous artists who used film, music, movement, and visual art to create a multimedia project that spoke of how their different indigenous nations shared common values but were distinctly their own. Curtis's goal for the collaborative project was to spark the viewers' awareness and hopefully start meaningful conversations about our experience with our own cultures.

Go Give It a Try!

Coming up with a new look doesn't mean you have to buy all new clothing. Using the clothes you already have, design a new look for yourself. Combine pieces you have never tried together before. Mix textures, solid colors, and prints to create a unique look that is entirely your own.

Henry Liang
Arts: Flutist

What if you became so interested in a new skill and then realized you were the only person in the country who could perform that skill? Wouldn't this make you want to inspire and share your talents with everyone? This is true for Henry Liang, a performer of the flute, the piccolo, and an instrument you may have never heard of before: the shō.

Early Musical Start

Henry was born in Guangzhou, China. At the age of six, he started playing the dizi, a wind instrument made of bamboo. Two years later, he picked up the flute. He had the opportunity to play with a youth orchestra in China before moving to Australia, where his dedication and love of music further developed with the guidance of exceptional teachers.

The Navy Band

In 2013 Henry enlisted as a musician in the Royal Australian Navy Band. The Navy Band has a long history in Australia and performs during significant ceremonies, engages the public with national pride, records albums of patriotic and original music, and upholds national traditions. Henry went to naval training and also practiced his music. He plays the flute and the piccolo with the band and has performed for many international leaders. From 2014 to 2017, Henry served as the president of the Flute Society of New South Wales.

The Shō

Henry became the only Australian musician actively specializing in the shō, a traditional Japanese wind instrument. The shō is made up of seventeen skinny bamboo pipes bundled together, whose history dates to the seventh century when it was used in Japanese royal courts. The musician breathes in and out through the mouthpiece to make sound with this unique instrument. In 2015 Henry traveled to Japan and studied the instrument with a leader in shō performance.

The Silkworm

The Australian Broadcasting Corporation provided funds for new Australian music to be created. This included Henry and his shō. Henry composed and recorded an album he created named *Mori*, which references the silkworm and is the Japanese word for "forest," the source of the bamboo used to make the shō. The musical suite has four movements or sections. Each represents a stage in a silkworm's life cycle and symbolizes our daily challenges and triumphs. When Henry was a child in China, he even had silkworms as pets; the creatures have a special place in his heart.

Practice

Even professionals such as exceptional artists, musicians, and athletes have to practice. This is true of Henry, who knows there are no shortcuts to achieving your best. With his instruments, he practices scales and long tones. A long tone is when you hold one note as long as possible while keeping a steady and clear tone. Even when the work can get frustrating, Henry relies on his love for creating and enjoying music to get him through.

Go Give It a Try!

Henry shares that musicians should not only practice, practice, practice, but they should also listen to lots of music all the time. Go online and search for "Henry Liang musician shō" to experience this unique musical instrument. Does this experience prompt you to want to try a new instrument?

Rufai Zakari

Arts: Visual Artist

Have you ever taken the time to consider how much trash you create in a day and where that trash ends up? Artist Rufai Zakari acknowledges our complicated relationship with the garbage we create and wants us to rethink what happens to our waste.

Toy Creator

Rufai was born in 1990 in Bawku, Ghana. As a kid, Rufai and his friends would collect pieces of garbage they found in the city streets. The kids would turn the collected bottles, food wrappers, and plastic bags into toys and sculptures.

Returning to Childhood

Rufai studied art in school, where he learned about painting techniques and then created street art with the mentorship of a well-known street artist. While using spray paint to create his work, he came across piles of garbage. These discarded materials sparked memories of his childhood when he would collect trash to create something new. He began including these found items in his artwork, exploring pollution and our role in its impact on our communities.

Portraits of Strength

The artworks Rufai creates are almost always portraits of women from his community. Their strength and resilience inspire him. He lovingly reimagines these women out of reclaimed materials. Rufai's portraits are created by stitching together the found plastic items, just as someone would sew pieces of fabric together to create a quilt. He doesn't hide that his art is made from found items but uses the colors and patterns found on plastic bottles and bags to create bold portraits.

Discovering Materials

When he first started repurposing trash, he would find the materials himself, and then his family members would help with the collecting. Now, he employs women and children in his community to help locate items, paying them for their efforts. Bawku, Rufai's hometown, has been deeply impacted by decades of conflict that left the city in ruins and resulted in many lost lives. But Rufai has hope for his community. He founded a nonprofit that pays community members for their efforts to find, clean, and provide materials for his artworks.

Global Conversations

Rufai's works are now exhibited in museums and galleries around the world. With his carefully stitched visuals, he can share his local community, the strength of its people, and our relationship with single-use plastics with the world.

Go Give It a Try!

Gather materials from your recycling bin or those ready to be thrown in the trash. Consider which ones you can work with safely and begin by playing with stacking, flattening, and folding the materials. Use limited additional materials (tape, glue, scissors) to assemble your found objects into sculptures.

Takeru "TK" Nagayoshi
Education: Teacher

An advocate is someone who publicly and boldly shows their support and recommends potential solutions or changes. An advocate sees something wrong and feels the need to use their voice and speak up. Takeru "TK" Nagayoshi found his voice and will continue using it to improve education for all students.

Lots of Change

TK was born on July 8, 1991, in New Jersey. His parents came to the United States from Tokyo. When he was nine, TK and his family moved to Japan because of his mom's job with the United Nations. In Japan, TK was faced with learning the Japanese language and attending a very different school setting than he was used to in the United States.

A New Challenge

At the age of fourteen, TK and his family came back to the United States. But now, he faced new challenges: His English language skills were rusty, and he lacked confidence in school. Thank goodness for great teachers who saw his potential and encouraged him throughout his learning.

Access to Diverse Literature

TK first studied international relations and then got a master's degree in education. He started teaching reading, writing, and research classes in Massachusetts. As an English teacher, TK thought back to the books he read when he was in high school. He realized that almost all the books were written by white men or featured main characters who were white. Characters of color were often minor characters. In the books he read in high school, he never encountered an Asian character, someone like himself. This truth led TK to provide his students with access to literature that was as diverse as the students in his classroom. He wanted to introduce all his students to the rich diversity of the human experience and to explore difficult topics together.

Advocacy through Writing

Advocacy became the cornerstone of TK's work. He advocated for excellent education for all students, specifically students of color. He wrote countless op-ed articles on education issues. An op-ed is a piece of writing that features the opinions of a knowledgeable author and are based on their lived experience. TK's writing was featured locally in Massachusetts and nationally.

Involvement and Recognition

TK believed in using his voice to advocate for students and teachers, and he would do just that. He served on committees, panels, and task forces centered on diversity and equity in education. Other media formats, such as webinars, podcasts, and radio interviews, helped him reach different audiences. He was named the 2020 Massachusetts Teacher of the Year in recognition of his efforts in and out of the classroom. He continues to write articles, book chapters, and op-eds that advocate for teachers and students, focusing on diversity and inclusion.

EDUCATION

Go Give It a Try!

Visit your local library and ask a librarian to help you find your favorite type of books (graphic novels, mystery, magical adventures, historical fiction, and so forth) that feature diverse main characters. You may find a new favorite character or even a new author to continue reading.

Tom Daley

Arts: Knitter

A gold medal Olympic athlete and accomplished knitter, Tom Daley has become a hero in the world of diving and also champions the powers of knitting. Armed with knitting needles, yarn, and a sense of purpose, Tom breaks outdated stereotypes of who can be an accomplished knitter.

Competitive Diving

Tom was born on May 21, 1994, in Plymouth, England. He started diving at the age of seven when a coach noticed his talents. He was then entered into national and international competitions. At fourteen, Tom was the youngest British competitor in the 2008 Summer Olympics. He competed in other Olympic games, winning gold and bronze medals. Tom had become a household name, and his stardom only increased with each appearance in and out of the pool.

Just Be Still

One of Tom's coaches approached him about his restlessness. Tom was told he was terrible at sitting still while resting and recovering. He needed to find a way just to be still. So, in March 2020 Tom decided to try out knitting. Knitting uses large needles and loops of yarn that interlace with other loops to create all kinds of clothing and soft accessories. During a trip to Canada, he watched YouTube videos. How hard could it be? But he couldn't get the hang of it. Australian and Russian divers offered advice and support, as well as one of the coaches on his British diving team. Only then did he start to grasp how to knit.

The Purple Scarf

The very first thing that Tom completed with his new knitting skills was a scarf for his mom. It was purple, her favorite color. It started terribly, but with focus, he gifted the scarf to his mom on Mother's Day. With time and practice, Tom became more confident, and his knitting skills strengthened. He could take on more challenging designs and forms, even coming up with his own designs. Knitting became his escape. When Tom got out his knitting needles, he became calm and focused.

Olympic Gold

Due to the COVID-19 pandemic, the 2020 Summer Olympics were held in 2021 in Tokyo. Because of the pandemic, no fans other than fellow athletes were welcome in the stands. On TV, the world saw Olympic diver Tom Daley in action—in the pool and with his knitting needles. While cheering on other athletes, Tom was spotted knitting away in the stands. He created a complicated cardigan sweater with Olympic rings and the British flag. In Tokyo, Tom won a gold medal for diving and knitted a small pouch for the medal. On one side was the U.K. flag, and on the other was the flag of Japan, the Olympic site for that year. He shared that he could carry his gold medal around without it getting scratched.

Go Give It a Try!

You don't need a complicated design or needles to start learning how to knit. Finger knitting requires yarn and your very own fingers. Watch tutorials online, and though it might be challenging at first, practice and perseverance can bring a sense of accomplishment and focus.

ARTS

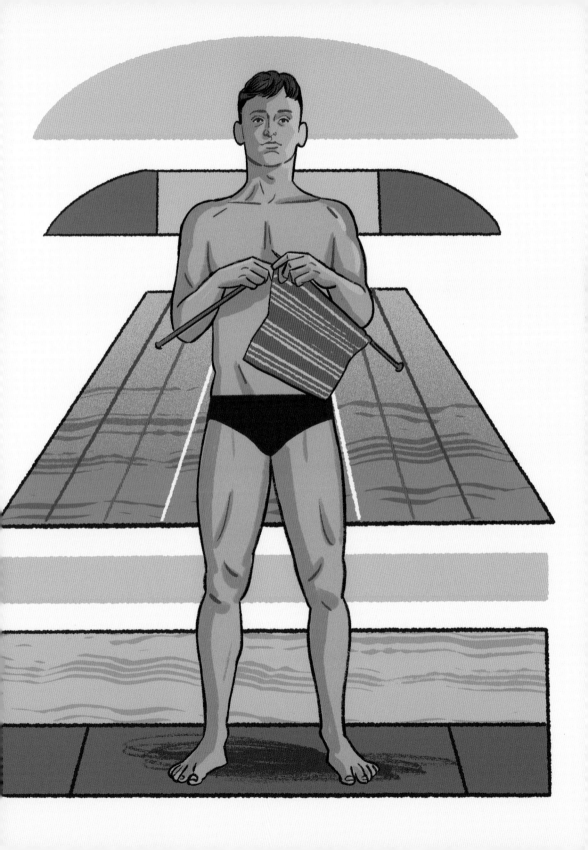

Kevin Aspaas

Arts: Weaver

Weaving is an art form that has roots in cultures and communities around the globe. The Navajo people, who prefer to be called the Diné ("The People"), have created weavings for centuries that connect them to the earth, their spirituality, and one another. Kevin Aspaas learned about weaving from his mother and honors his family legacy while making work that is all his own.

Weaving a Connection

Kevin was born in 1995 in New Mexico. When he was around eight years old, his mother began to teach him how to weave. She had learned from her sister, who had learned from their mother. Kevin started by learning how to weave simple sash belts. Weaving is a traditional art form in the Diné community, but not just an art form. Weaving provides warmth, clothing, and a connection to the earth and their ancestors. Kevin sat and heard stories about his grandmother as he learned to weave.

Weaving a Legacy

Weaving is an important part of Diné culture and history. Many generations ago, both men and women took part in weaving, but European settlers had more rigid gender systems and most recent weavers were women. When Kevin was a kid, he focused only on the weaving. He didn't know much about the rich culture and history associated with the art he was creating. Elders in his community taught him the importance of weaving beyond its beauty. Kevin decided to become a weaver to continue the legacy of his family of weavers, craftspeople, and storytellers.

Sheep-to-Loom

Kevin's grandmother owned a flock of sheep, which she cared for, and used their wool to create her weavings. In 2020, after learning weaving from his family, Kevin became dedicated to the traditional Navajo sheep-to-loom weaving process. He moved to Shiprock, New Mexico, on the Navajo Nation. Here, he has a flock of sheep that rely on him for their care. The seasons dictate the sheep's needs, and their care is reflected in the wool. Kevin knows that the weavings made from his sheep's wool will be stronger, more vibrant, and more powerful as he cares for them. But it isn't just the wool that he collects naturally. Kevin uses found natural materials to create his own dyes to make different colored wool for his weavings.

The Art

Navajo weavings grew in popularity after the railroad expanded through the Southwest in the late nineteenth century. However, only specific woven designs were deemed most marketable by traders. So, the Navajo weavers were limited in what they created and neglected traditional patterns. Kevin worked with another skilled weaver to learn these traditional designs and methods, incorporating them into his work. Beyond woven works of art that collectors and museums value, Kevin believes in the power of making works for others. He weaves traditional dresses, belts, and moccasins for members of his broader community.

ARTS

Go Give It a Try!

Research how to make your own natural dyes with the plants and vegetables you have around the house. Search for tutorials online that explain which plants produce different colors. Test out your new dyes on white fabric and consider dying white T-shirts. Use a fixative to set the dyes so that they won't wash out.

Adrian Bermudez
Health: Nurse

Look around at the adults in your life. Are they your role models? Do they set a standard for you to follow? This was true for Adrian Bermudez, who saw in his family members the challenges and triumphs of caring for others. He saw possibilities for himself and now supports others to do the same.

Family Inspiration
Adrian was born in 1997 in New York City. He grew up in East Brunswick, New Jersey, with inspiring nurses in his life. His mom was an intensive care unit (ICU) nurse in New York, and his grandma was a nursing director at a nursing home in New Jersey.

Baseball Injury
When Adrian was ten years old, he suffered a dramatic baseball injury. He had a torn shoulder labrum, an injury that is like the kind that Major League Baseball players can get. He was the youngest patient the surgeon had ever seen with this injury. Adrian had to spend lots of time in the hospital during and after the surgery with many doctors and nurses. Spending so much time in the hospital at an early age sparked his interest in the medical field.

Men in Nursing Club
Adrian went on to study nursing at the University of Pittsburgh. While there, Adrian cofounded the university's first Men in Nursing Club. The club would become a place for male nursing students to connect, find mentorship, and recruit others to join nursing. Mentorship, when someone with lots of experience provides guidance and support to someone with less experience, is really important to Adrian. Throughout nursing school, he had the mentorship of his family and the upperclassmen who had been through the program. He knew he wanted to pay it forward by making mentorship a priority of the new Men in Nursing Club.

Hands-on Learning
Exciting others about the nursing field, especially other young men, is important to Adrian and inspired him to take their club on the road. He and some of the club's members started visiting local Pittsburgh high schools to answer questions about what being a nurse is like. After the discussion, the students were then able to participate in hands-on learning about nursing skills. Students could meet with college admission counselors about what it would take to get involved in a nursing program. Adrian's goal of exciting others about nursing was coming true.

COVID-19
COVID-19 changed life for everyone, but especially for those in health care. Adrian worked alongside his mom in the same New York City ICU during the COVID-19 pandemic: two nurses, mother and son, working to care for vulnerable patients at the same hospital where Adrian was born. For Adrian, it has always been about connecting with patients when they may be experiencing the worst days of their life.

Go Give It a Try!
Check out clubs that are available for you to join at your school or within your local community based on your interests. You could find a new group of like-minded people. If you are looking for a club that doesn't exist, it is time to start one. Think about the purpose of your club, what you would accomplish together, and what adult support may be needed to make it all possible.

Acknowledgments

This project would not have been possible without Richard Reeve's research and H.E.A.L. concept that challenges us to rethink stereotypes and possibilities. May this book serve as an inspirational resource to introduce our children to male role models in the fields of health, education, arts, and literacy who have made this world a more empathetic and beautiful place. To the men who are featured in this book, thank you for your work and for stepping into spaces with confidence, curiosity, and creativity. Thank you for sharing rich, vulnerable stories of your lived experiences. I am certain that your profiles will inspire future leaders and dreamers.

Thank you to Jonathan Simcosky and the Quarry Books team for their guidance throughout this process, and their dedication to this project. Endless gratitude to Chris King who breathed life into these profiles with his beautifully expressive portraits. And to my family, thank you for your unwavering support throughout all the seasons of our life together.

—Jonathan Juravich

About the Authors

Jonathan Juravich began teaching elementary art outside of Columbus, Ohio, in 2005. Still actively teaching art to young students, his personal and professional focus is on the importance of social and emotional learning in our daily lives. This is his favorite topic for research and discussion, including his PhD dissertation, his TED Talk "How Do We Teach Empathy," his limited-series podcast *The Art of SEL*, and his Emmy award–winning digital drawing program "Drawing with Mr. J." In 2018, Jonathan was named Ohio Teacher of the Year and one of four finalists for National Teacher of the Year. In 2023, he was named the National Elementary Art Teacher of the Year by the National Art Education Association. He lives in Columbus, Ohio, with his family.

Richard V. Reeves is the founding president of the American Institute for Boys and Men (AIBM) and the author of *Of Boys and Men: Why the Modern Male Is Struggling, Why It Matters, and What to Do about It.* Before founding AIBM in 2023, Richard was a senior fellow at the Brookings Institution. While at Brookings, he focused on policies related to economic inequality, racial justice, social mobility, and boys and men. He is also a regular contributor to the *New York Times*, the *Atlantic*, *National Affairs*, and other publications.

Between 2010 and 2012, Richard was director of strategy to the United Kingdom's Deputy Prime Minister. A former European Business Speaker of the Year, his other previous roles include director of Demos, the London-based political think tank, principal policy advisor to the Minister for Welfare Reform, research fellow at the Institute for Public Policy Research, and journalist for the *Guardian* and *Observer* newspapers. He earned a BA from Oxford University and a PhD from Warwick University. Richard tweets from @richardvreeves and his website is richardvreeves.com.

About the Illustrator

Chris King is an illustrator and artist from West Yorkshire, in the north of England, whose illustrations have an impactful style based on strong line work and a lifelong love for comic books. His figurative illustrations have led him to work for leading media outlets, publishing houses and consumer brands worldwide. When not drawing Chris can be found making music and walking the many moorland trails near his home.

Index